INCREASING CYBER CRIMES IN INDIA

ARITRA MONDAL

notionpress.com

INDIA • SINGAPORE • MALAYSIA

ISBN 979-8-89233-892-9

"In the ever-advancing realm of technology, the
shadow of cybercrime grows longer, reminding us that
progress must be met with equal measures of vigilance
and innovation in defense."

Contents

CHAPTER 1

Introduction

Hi! I'm Aritra. Today I am here to discuss on the topic "Increasing Cybercrimes in India".

Before diving into the topic let me give you a brief idea about the topic.

In recent years, India has witnessed a concerning and rapid surge in cybercrimes, creating a growing challenge for law enforcement agencies, businesses and individuals alike. This digital age has brought unprecedented connectivity and convenience to the life of millions, but it has also opened the door to host cyber threats and criminal activities. As technology continues to advance and the internet becomes an integral part of everyday life, the nation finds itself grappling with an alarming increase in cybercrimes that span a wide spectrum of illicit activities. This essay will delve into the factors contributing to the rise in cybercrimes in India, the various forms these crimes take and the implications they have on society, the economy and national security. Furthermore, it will explore the measures taken by the Indian government and law enforcement agencies to address this growing menace and protect the digital landscape. Understanding the dynamics of cybercrimes in India is crucial in order to develop effective strategies for prevention, detection, and prosecution in the ever-evolving cyber threat landscape. The increasing cybercrimes in India can be attributed to a combination of factors, including technological advancements, greater internet-penetration, evolving criminal tactics and socio economic factors.

1.1 Understanding the Digital Age

Understanding the digital age is multifaceted concept that encompasses the profound impact of digital technology on nearly every aspect of modern society. It involves recognizing and comprehending the transformative changes brought about by the widespread adoption and integration of digital technology into our daily lives, economies and institutions. Here's a breakdown of key aspects to consider when trying to understand the digital age:

1. **Technological Advancements:** The digital age is characterized by rapid advancements in digital technologies, including but not limited to computers and the Internet of Things<IoT). These technologies have not only become pervasive but also highly interconnected.

2. **Data as a Driver:** Data has emerged as a critical driver of the digital age. With the ability to collect, process, and analyze vast amounts of data, individuals, organizations, and governments can make more informed decisions, improve efficiency and develop new products and services.

3. **Global Connectivity:** The internet has connected people, business, and governments worldwide, enabling instant communication, information sharing, and global collaboration. This interconnectedness has revolutionized various industries and has blurred the boundaries between nations.

4. **Digital Transformation:** Many industries and sections have undergone a process of digital transformation, which involves reimagining traditional practices and processes using digital technological. This can include everything from e-commerce and telemedicine to smart cities and digital banking.

5. **Social and Cultural Changes:** The digital age has reshaped social interactions and cultural norms. Social media platforms have become major channels for communication, entertainment, and self-expression, influencing how people

from relationships, share information, and engage in public discourse.

6. **E-commerce:** Digitalization has revolutionized commerce with e-commerce platforms. Understanding this aspect involves grasping the shift from brick-and-mortar retail to online shopping and its impact on business and consumers.

7. **Digital Culture:** The digital age has given rise to unique digital culture, characterized by online communities, digital art, memes, and internet subcultures. Understanding this culture is essential for comprehending modern social dynamics.

8. **Privacy and Security:** In the digital age, concerns about data privacy and cybersecurity are paramount. Understanding this involves being aware of the risks associated with digital interactions and the measures to mitigate them.

9. **Digital Literacy:** Being digitally literate is crucial in the digital age. This includes not only knowing how to use digital tools but also understanding digital ethics and discerning reliable information from misinformation.

10. **Artificial Intelligence (AI) and Automation:** AI and automation are reshaping industries and the workforce. Understanding the digital age involves appreciating how IoT applications such as smart homes and smart cities, are changing daily.

In summary, understanding the digital age is about acknowledging the far-reaching consequences of digital technology and the internet on society, economy, culture, and individual behavior. It involves being aware of both the opportunities and challenges that come with living in an increasingly digital and connected world. This era is marked by global connectivity, vast data generation, and unprecedented access to information. In this era, individuals and organizations must adapt to the opportunities and challenges posed by an increasingly interconnected and technologically driven world.

1.2 The Proliferation of Technology India

The topic "The Proliferation of Technology in India" refers to the widespread adoption and growth of technology and digital infrastructure within the Indian subcontinent. Over the past few decades, India has witnessed a remarkable transformation in various sections, driven by advancements in technology. Here are some key points to help explain this topic:

1. **Digital Revolution:** India has experienced a digital revolution, with significant progress in areas such as telecommunications, internet access, and mobile technology. This has led to increased connectivity across the country, even in rural areas.

2. **Smartphone Penetration:** The proliferation of affordable smartphones has been a game-changer. Millions of Indians now have access to the internet and a wide range of digital services through their smartphones.

3. **Internet Access:** The growth of technology in India has led to increased internet penetration. Internet access is no longer limited to urban areas, as it has expanded to rural regions through initiatives like Digital India.

4. **E-Governance:** The Indian government has also adopted the e governance initiatives to provide digital services to citizens. This includes online portals for services like applying for government documents, paying taxes, and accessing information.

5. **Start-up Ecosystem:** India has seen the emergence of a vibrant start-up ecosystem, especially in technology driven sectors like e-commerce, fintech, health tech, and edtech. These start-ups have attracted significant investments and created job opportunities.

6. **Digital Payments:** The proliferation of technology has led to a surge in digital payment methods, such as mobile

wallets, net banking, UPI (Unified Payment Interface), transforming the way people conduct financial transactions.

7. **Digital Education:** The COVID-19 pandemic accelerated the adoption of digital education in India. E-learning platforms, online classes, and digital resources have become essential for students and educators.

8. **Digital Inclusion:** Efforts have been made to ensure digital inclusion, bridging the digital divide by providing affordable devices and internet access to marginalized communities.

9. **IT Services:** India is known as a global hub for IT services and software development. Indian IT companies play in crucial role in providing technology solutions to business worldwide.

10. **Digital Innovation:** India has become a hotbed for innovation, with a focus on emerging technologies like artificial intelligence, blockchain, and data analytics.

11. **Digital Challenges:** Alongside the proliferation of technology, India faces challenges such as cybersecurity threats, data privacy concerns, and the need for robust digital infrastructure in remote areas.

12. **Impact on Society:** The proliferation of technology in India has had a profound impact on society, affecting how people communicate, work, shop, learn, and access healthcare.

In summary, the proliferation of technology in India represents a transformative shift that has touched every aspect of Indian life. It has not only improved access to services and information but also created new economic opportunities and driven innovation. However, it also comes with challenges that need to be addressed to ensure that the benefits of technology are accessible to all segments of society.

1.3 Defining Cybercrimes

Cybercrimes, also known as computer crimes or internet crimes, refer to unlawful activities committed using digital technology, computer systems, or the internet. These crimes involve the use of technology to perpetrate illegal activities, often with the intent to cause harm, steal data, defraud, or disrupt computer systems and networks. To understand the topic of defining cybercrimes, it's essential to explore the key elements, types, and implications of these offenses.

Key elements of Defining Cyber Crimes:

1. **Digital Medium:** Cybercrimes are fundamentally dependent on digital technology. They are committed to using computers, the internet, or other electronic devices as a means to facilitate illegal actions.

2. **Illegality:** Cybercrimes involve actions that are prohibited by law. These can range from unauthorized access to computer systems to online harassment or financial fraud.

3. **Intent:** In many cases, cybercrimes are committed with malicious intent. Perpetrators often aim to achieve financial gain, steal sensitive information, damage reputations, or disrupt systems.

4. **Concealment:** Cybercriminals often use sophisticated techniques to hide their identity or location, making it challenging for law enforcement agencies to track them down.

Common types of Cyber Crimes:

1. **Hacking:** Unauthorized access to computer systems, networks, or websites for various purposes, including data theft, data manipulation, or simply_ causing disruption.

2. **Malware:** The creation and distribution of malicious software, such as viruses, worms, Trojans, ransomware, and spyware, with the intent to compromise computer systems or steal data.

3. **Phishing:** Deceptive emails or websites that trick individuals into revealing sensitive information, like passwords or financial details, often used for identity theft or fraud.

4. **Identity Theft:** Stealing someone's personal information to assume their identity for fraudulent purposes, such as accessing a bank account or committing financial fraud.

5. **Online Fraud:** Committing fraud or scams online, which can include online auctions fraud, credit card fraud, and investment scams.

6. **Cyberbullying:** Using digital platforms to harass, threaten, or intimidate individuals, often through social media or messaging apps.

7. **Cyber Espionage:** Illegally obtaining sensitive information, trade secrets, or government secrets through digital means for economic, political, or military advantage.

8. **Distributed Denial of Service (DDoS) Attacks:** Overloading a target's computer system or network with excessive traffic, rendering it temporarily or permanently inaccessible.

Implications and Challenges:

1. **Security Concerns:** Cybercrimes pose significant security risks to individuals, business, and governments. They can result in financial losses, data breaches, and damage to reputations.

2. **Global Nature:** Cybercrimes often cross international borders, making it difficult to track and prosecute offenders. This requires international cooperation in addressing these crimes.

3. **Privacy Invasion:** Many cybercrimes involve the violation of individual's privacy, such as the unauthorized collection of personal data or surveillance.

4. **Economic Impact:** The financial consequences of cybercrimes are substantial, with business and individuals suffering losses in the billions of dollars each year.

5. **Legal Frameworks:** Defining and prosecuting cybercrimes require continually evolving legal frameworks and international agreements to keep pace with technological advancements.

6. **Prevention and Awareness:** Education and awareness campaigns are essential to help individuals and organizations protect themselves against cyber threats.

In conclusion, defining cybercrimes involves recogn1z1ng illegal activities committed through digital technology and understanding their various forms and potential consequences. As technology continues to advance, the definition of cybercrimes will also evolve, making it crucial for law enforcement, governments, and individuals to stay informed and proactive in addressing these digital threats.

CHAPTER 2

The Landscape of Cybercrime in India

The landscape of cybercrime in India has evolved significantly in recent years, reflecting both the rapid digitalization of the country and the emergence of new challenges and threats. As one of the world's most populous and technologically advancing nations, India has become a fertile ground for cybercriminal activities. This introductory overview delves into the complex and dynamic realm of cybercrime in India, outlining its various facets, the evolving nature of threats, the legal and security frameworks in place, and the socio-economic implications on the nation as a whole. Understanding the landscape of cybercrime 1n India 1s essential for policymakers, law enforcement agencies, businesses, and individuals as they navigate the digital age while safeguarding against potential risks and vulnerabilities.

2.1 Historical Perspective

A historical perspective on the landscape of cybercrime in India provides insights into how cybercrimes have evolved and the various factors that have shaped this complex arena over three years. Here's an overview of the historical development of cybercrime in India:

1. **Emergence of Computers (Pre-2000s):**

   In the pre-2000s era, India saw a gradual adoption of computers in government, businesses, and households.

   The early use of computers primarily involved basic office work and data processing, with limited internet connectivity.

2. **Pioneering Cyber Laws (Early 2000s):**

   India recognized the need for legal frameworks to address cybercrimes and enacted the Information Technology (IT) Act in 2000.

   This legislation provided the first legal definitions and penalties for cybercrimes and established the CERT-In (Indian Computer Emergency Response Team) to handle cybersecurity incidents.

3. **Growth of Internet and E-commerce (Mid-2000s):**

   The mis-2000s saw significant growth in internet penetration and e-commerce in India.

   As more people and businesses went online, cybercrimes related to fraud, data breaches, and online scams started to rise.

4. **Sophistication of Cyber Attacks (Late 2000s-Early 2010s):**

   Cybercriminals began to employ more sophisticated techniques, including malware, phishing, and distributed denial of service (DDoS) attacks.

High-profile cases of cyber espionage and attacks on critical infrastructure were reported.

5. **Digital Payments and Financial Crimes (Mid-2010s)**

The advent of digital payment systems, mobile wallets, and online banking led to a surge in financial cybercrimes, such as online fraud and identity theft.

The government's "Digital India" initiative aimed to boost the digital economy but also posed new security challenges.

6. **Data Privacy and Data Protection (Late 2010s):**

Concerns about data privacy and data protection gained prominence as large-scale data breaches and the misuse of personal data made headlines.

The General Data Protection Regulation (GDPR) and discussions about India's own data protection laws highlighted the need for stronger cybersecurity measures.

7. **Social Media and Online Harassment (Late 2010s-Present)**

The use of social media platforms. brought issues like cyberbullying, online harassment, and the spread of fake news to the forefront.

These concerns have led to discussions about regulating social media platforms.

8. **COVID-19 and New Cyber Threats (2020s)**

The COVID-19 pandemic accelerated digital transformation, making remote work and online education the new normal.

Cybercriminals exploited pandemic-related vulnerabilities, leading to an increase in phishing attacks, ransomware incidents, and telehealth-related fraud.

9. **Legislative Revisions and Cybersecurity Initiatives (Ongoing)**

India has continued to update its cyber laws, most notably with the Personal Data Protection Bill.

The government has also launched initiatives like the National Cyber Security Strategy to enhance cybersecurity and protect critical infrastructure.

A historical perspective on the landscape of cybercrime in India underscores the dynamic nature of the field, as technology advances and cybercriminals adapt to new opportunities and challenges. The evolving legal and security frameworks, along with increased awareness, play a crucial role in addressing cyber threats and securing India's digital landscape.

2.2 Current Trends and Statistics

Understanding the current trends and statistics on the landscape of cybercrime in India provides valuable insights into the evolving nature of cyber threats and their impact on the country. Here is an overview of the latest trends and statistics:

1. **Rising Incidence of Cybercrimes:**

   Cybercrime incidents in India have been on the rise in recent years, reflecting the increasing reliance on digital technology and internet connectivity.

2. **Financial Cybercrimes:**

   Financial cybercrimes, such as online fraud, identity theft, and phishing attacks, remain a significant concern. India has seen a surge financial crime targeting individuals and business.

3. **Cyberattacks on Critical Infrastructure:**

   Critical infrastructure, including power grids, healthcare systems, and financial institutions, is at risk from cyberattacks. Such incidents can have far reaching consequences for the nation's security and economy.

4. **Ransomware Attacks:**

   Ransomware attacks, where cybercriminals encrypt data and demand a ransom for its release, have become more prevalent. These attacks often target businesses and government organizations.

5. **Online Harassment and Cyberbullying:**

   With the increased use of social media and online platforms, cases of online harassment, cyberbullying, and the spread of fake news have grown. These issues have to led to discussions about regulating social media.

6. **Data Breaches:**

High-profile data breaches have exposed the personal information of millions of individuals, leading to concerns about data privacy and the need for stronger data protection regulations

7. **COVID-19 Related Cyber Threats:**

The COVID-19 pandemic has created new opportunities for cybercriminals. They have exploited vulnerabilities related to remote work, online education, and telehealth, resulting in an increase in pandemic related cyber threats.

8. **E-commerce and Online Scams:**

With the growth of e-commerce in India, online scams related to fake product listings, counterfeit goods, and fraudulent online marketplaces have become more common.

9. **Legislative Departments:**

India is actively working on legislation to address data pnvacy concerns. The Personal Data Protection Bill and discussions surrounding India's data protection laws highlight efforts to strengthen cybersecurity and protect personal data.

10. **National Cybersecurity Initiatives:**

The government of India has launched the National Cyber Security Strategy and other initiatives to enhance cybersecurity, protect critical infrastructure, and promote cybersecurity awareness and education.

11. **International Cooperation:**

Cybercrimes often transcend borders, making international cooperation crucial in addressing cyber threats and prosecuting cybercriminals.

Statistics related to cybercrime in India can vary, and up-to-date data is essential for a comprehensive understanding of the current landscape. These statistics include the number of reported cybercrimes, financial losses incurred, the sectors most targeted by cyberattacks, and the success rates of cybersecurity measures and law enforcement efforts.

In summary the current trends and statistics on the landscape of cybercrime in India reflect a complex and evolving environment. As digital technology continues to advance, addressing cyber threats, and enhancing cybersecurity measures remain critical for safeguarding India's digital landscape and protecting individuals, businesses, and critical infrastructure from cybercriminal activities.

2.3 High-Profile Cases

High-profile cases on the landscape of cybercrime in India represent notable incidents of cybercrimes that have garnered significant attention dur to their scale, impact, or the nature of the offenses involved. These cases provide insights into the evolving challenges and complexities of cybersecurity in the country. Here are some examples of high-profile cybercrime cases in India:

1. **Uno coin Bitcoin ATM Case (2018):**

   Uno coin, a cryptocurrency exchange, installed India's first Bitcoin ATM in Bengaluru.

   The installation led to legal issues, as cryptocurrencies operated in a regulatory grey area at the time. The founders of Uno coin were arrested, highlighting the regulatory challenges surrounding digital currencies.

2. **Aadhaar Data Leak (2017-2018):**

   India's Aadhaar system, which holds the biometric and personal data of over a billion citizens, faced multiple security breaches.

   These incidents raised concerns about data privacy and the security of the Aadhar database, leading to debates on the need for comprehensive data protection laws.

3. **WannaCry Ransomware Attack (2017):**

   The global WannaCry ransomware attack affected organizations worldwide, including in India.

   Hospitals, banks, and government agencies in India faced disruptions, emphasizing the need for robust cybersecurity measures in critical sectors.

4. **Nirav Modi PNB Bank Fraud (2018):**

   This financial fraud case involved the fraudulent issuance of letters of undertaking by jeweler Nirav Modi and his associates, leading to a massive loss for Punjab National Bank (PNB).

Although not a cyberattack in the tradition. sense, it highlighted the importance of securing financial systems and preventing digital fraud.

5. **AgustaWestland Scandal (2016):**

The Indian Air Force's VVIP helicopter deal was embroiled in allegations of corruption.

Hacked emails and electronic records played a role in uncovering the corruption scandal, demonstrating how digital evidence can shape high-profile cases.

6. **ISRO Espionage Case (1994):**

This case involved the illegal transfer of classified documents from the Indian Space Research Organisation0SRO) to foreign entities.

It underscored the national security risks associated with cyber espionage and data breaches.

7. **Mumbai Power Outage (2020):**

A large-scale power outage in Mumbai was attributed to a cyberattack on the electrical grid.

This incident highlighted the vulnerability of critical infrastructure to cyber threats and the need for enhanced security measures.

8. **Pegasus Spyware Controversy (2021):**

The use of the Pegasus spyware for surveillance purposes in India raised concerns about the potential abuse of surveillance tools and their impact on individual privacy.

These high-profile cases in the landscape of cybercrime in India encompass a range of cyber threats, from financial fraud and data breaches to cyber espionage and ransomware attacks. They serve as reminders of the need for robust cybersecurity measures, effective law enforcement, and regulatory frameworks to address the ever evolving challenges in the digital age. Moreover, they highlight the importance of public and private sector vigilance in protecting critical infrastructure and sensitive information.

CHAPTER 3

The Motive Behind Cybercrimes

The motives behind cybercrimes are diverse and often driven by a combination of factors that lead individuals or groups to engage in illegal activities within the digital realm. Understanding these motives is essential to combat cybercrimes effectively. Here are some common motives behind cybercrimes:

1. **Financial Gain:**

   Financial motives are among the most prevalent in the world of cybercrimes. Perpetrators seek to make money through various means, such as:

   - **Online Fraud:** Committing scams and frauds to obtain money or goods, including phishing, identity theft, and advance-free fraud.

   - **Ransomware:** Encrypting a victim's data and demanding a ransom in exchange for the decryption key.

   - **Credit Card Theft:** Stealing credit card details and using them for unauthorized transactions.

   - **Cyber Extortion:** Threatening individuals or organizations with exposure of sensitive information unless a ransom paid.

2. **Hacktivism:**

   Some individuals or groups engage in cybercrimes to advance a particular ideology, political agenda, or social cause:

   - **Distributed Denial of Service (DDoS):** Overloading websites or networks to disrupt services, often as a form of protest or activism.

   - **Data Breaches:** Exposing confidential information to highlight perceived injustices or corruption.

3. **Espionage and Intelligence Gathering:**

   Nation-states, intelligence agencies, and corporate espionage groups engage in cybercrimes to gather sensitive information:

   - **Cyber Espionage:** Illegally accessing confidential data, trade secrets or government information for national security or economic advantage.

   - **Corporate Espionage:** Targeting business rivals to obtain their proprietary information, intellectual property, or strategies.

4. **Revenge or Malice:**

   Some cybercrimes are motivated by personal vendettas, harassment, or a desire to cause harm to others:

   - **Cyberbullying:** Harassing individuals online, causing emotional distress.

   - **Online Harassment:** Targeting victims with threats, hate speech, or intimidation.

   - **Doxing:** Publishing personal information about individuals with malicious intent.

5. **Thrill-Seeking and Notoriety:**

   A subset of cybercriminals seeks excitement and recognition:

   - **Vandalism and Defacement:** Hacking websites or networks to leave their mark and gain notoriety.

- **Creating Malware:** Developing and distributing malware for the challenge and recognition it brings.

6. **Information Brokerage:**

Some cybercriminals steal and sell sensitive data, including personal information, to the highest bidder on the dark web.

7. **Competitive Advantage:**

Business may engage in cybercrimes to gain a competitive edge over their rivals:

- **Corporate Sabotage:** Disrupting a competitor's operations or stealing their proprietary information.

8. **Economic Factors:**

Socioeconomic factors, such as unemployment poverty, and financial desperation, can lead individuals to commit cybercrimes as a means of financial survival.

9. **Inadequate Cybersecurity Knowledge:**

Some cybercrimes occur due to lack of awareness, accidental actions, or negligence, rather than malicious intent. For instance, users who inadvertently click on malicious links or download infected files.

Understanding the motives behind cybercrimes is essential for law enforcements, cybersecurity experts, and policymakers in developing strategies to prevent and respond to these offences effectively. Cybercrimes continue to evolve as technology advances, requiring ongoing efforts to address these threats and protect individuals, organizations, and critical infrastructure in the digital age.

3.1 Financial Gain

"Financial gain" is one of the primary and most common motives behind cybercrimes. Cybercriminals engage in various illegal activities with the intent of making money. Here's a more detailed explanation of how financial gain plays a central role in motivating cybercrimes:

1. **Types of Cybercrimes for Financial Gain**

   Online Fraud: Cybercriminals employ various fraudulent schemes to deceive individuals or organizations and obtain money or valuable assets. These schemes include:

   - **Phishing:** Sending deceptive emails or messages that appear to be from reputable sources to trick individuals into revealing sensitive financial information, such as login credentials and credit card details.

   - **Advance Fee Fraud:** Con artists.promise money in exchange for an upfront victims large sums of fee,which is never delivered as promised.

   - **Investment Fraud:** Offering fake investment opportunities with the promise of high returns, luring victims to invest money.

   - **Ransomware:** This type of cybercrime involves encrypting a victim's data or computer system and demanding a ransom to provide the decryption key. Victims, often business or individuals, are forced to pay to regain access to their data.

   - **Credit Card Theft:** Cybercriminals steal credit card details through various means, including data breaches, skimming devices, or phishing attacks. They then use these stolen details for unauthorized transactions, often selling the information on underground forums.

   - **Cyber Extortion:** In cases of cyber extortion, criminals threaten to release sensitive information or harm a victim's online reputation unless a ransom is paid. These threats often target individuals, businesses, or public figures.

2. **Malware Distribution:** Cybercriminals create and distribute malware with the goal of financial gain. This can involve:

   • **Banking Trojans:** Malware that targets online banking systems to steal login credentials and financial data.

   • **Crypto jacking:** Illegally using victim's computer resources to mine cryptocurrencies, which are then sent to the criminal wallet.

3. **Monetary Impact:**

   • The financial impact of cybercrimes can be devasting. Victims often suffer significant monetary losses, including stolen funds, fraudulent charges, ransom payment, and the costs associated with resolving cybercrimes.

4. **Anonymous Transactions:**

   • The internet allows cybercriminals to remain relatively anonymous. Transactions can be conducted using cryptocurrency, which offers a level of anonymity and makes it challenging for authorities to trace the flow of funds.

5. **Profit Motive:**

   • The profit motive is a driving force behind financial cybercrimes. Cybercriminals are motivated by the potential for substantial financial rewards with a lower risk of being caught compared to traditional criminal activities.

6. **Global Reach:**

   • Cybercrimes for financial gain are not limited by geographical boundaries. Criminals can target victims around the world, making it challenging for law enforcement to combat these crimes effectively.

Understanding the motive of financial gain in cybercrimes 1s essential for individuals, business, and law enforcement agencies to take proactive measures to protect themselves against cyber threats. This includes implementing robust cybersecurity measures, educating users about online security best practices, and reporting cybercrimes to appropriate authorities to enhance cybercrime prevention and response efforts.

3.2 Espionage and State-Sponsored Attacks

Espionage and state-sponsored cyberattacks are a category of cybercrimes in which governments or state entities engage 1n hacking, cyber-espionage, or other malicious online activities to gather intelligence, exert influence, or pursue national interests. These activities are often clandestine, with the primary goal of acquiring sensitive information from other nations, organizations, or individuals. Here's a more detailed explanation of this topic:

Espionage in the Digital Age:

1. **State-Sponsored Espionage:** Governments have a long history of conducting espionage to gather information for political, military, or economic advantages. In the digital age, state-sponsored espionage has moved to cyberspace, with nations deploying cyber capabilities to collect data and intelligence from foreign entities.

2. **Cyber Espionage:** This involves hacking into the networks and systems of foreign governments, corporations, or individuals to steal sensitive information. Such data can include defense plans, trade secrets, intellectual property, diplomatic communications, and more.

3. **Advanced Persistent Threats (APTs):** State-sponsored cyber espionage often involves APTs, which are sophisticated and long term cyberattacks aimed at a specific target. These attacks can be ongoing for months or even years, allowing the attackers to gain deep access and steal data discreetly.

4. **Motivations for State-Sponsored Espionage:**

   Governments engage 1n cyber espionage for. various reasons, including:

   - **National Security:** Gathering intelligence on potential threats and adversaries.

- **Economic Gain:** Stealing trade secrets and intellectual property to gain a competitive edge.

- **Diplomatic Advantage:** Monitoring diplomatic negotiations and other nation's strategies.

- **Counterterrorism:** Tracking terrorist organizations and their activities

State-Sponsored Cyber Attacks:

1. **Cyber-attacks carried out or supported by nation-states:** In addition to espionage, governments may launch cyber-attacks that cause disruption, damage, or chaos, often to further national interests. These attacks can target critical infrastructure, military system, or financial institutions.

2. **Stuxnet:** An infamous example of a state-sponsored cyber-attack is the Stuxnet worm, believed to be developed by the U.S. and Israel. Stuxnet was designed to sabotage Iran's nuclear program by causing physical damage to centrifuge in its nuclear facilities.

3. **NotPetya:** Another well-known example is the NotPetya ransomware attack, which initially appeared as a ransom attack but is believed to have been state-sponsored, with Russia being the primary suspect. It caused widespread damage to critical infrastructure and business.

4. **Motivations for State-Sponsored Cyber Attacks:** State-sponsored cyber-attacks can serve multiple purposes:

   - **Military and Defence:** Disrupting or degrading an adversary's military capabilities.

   - **Political Manipulation:** Influencing elections, spreading propaganda, or undermining foreign governments.

   - **Economic Warfare:** Targeting a nation's economic infrastructure to cause financial harm or gain leverage in trade negotiations.

5. **Attribution Challenges:** One of the major challenges in state sponsored cyber incidents is attributing the attack to a specific nation-state. Attackers often take steps to hide their identities, and some cyber operations are highly classified and conducted through third parties.

Understanding espionage and state-sponsored attacks is crucial for governments, businesses, and individuals to protect sensitive information, bolster cybersecurity measures, and engage in diplomatic efforts to prevent and respond to such cyber threats. These activities continue to evolve and pose significant challenges to the security and stability of nations in the digital age.

3.3 Ideological and Hacktivist Motivations

"Ideological and hacktivist motivations" refer to the underlying beliefs, principles, and causes that drive individuals or groups to engage in hacktivist activities. Hacktivism is a form of cyber activism that involves using hacking and digital skills to advance a particular ideology, advocate for social or political change, or protest against perceived injustices. Here's an explanation of ideological and hacktivist motivations:

1. **Ideological Motivations:**

   - **Political Ideology:** Some hacktivists are motivated by political ideologies. They may support a specific political movement, party, or cause and use hacking as a means to further their agenda. This can include actions such as defacing websites or disrupting online services of political opponents.

   - **Social Justice:** Ideological hacktivists may be driven by a desire for social justice. They may target organizations or individuals they believe are perpetuating social injustices, inequality, or discrimination. Hacking actions could include exposing sensitive information or conducting cyber campaigns to raise awareness.

   - **Environmental Activism:** Some hacktivists are passionate about environmental causes and may target corporations or institutions they see s contributing to. environmental harm. Hacking actions may involve exposing environmental violations or disrupting operations.

   - **Anti-Corporate or Anti-Capitalist Beliefs:** Hacktivists with anti-corporate or anti-capitalist ideologies may target businesses they view as exploitative or unethical. Their actions can include website defacement or leaking internal documents to expose corporate misconduct.

- **Freedom of Information:** Hacktivists who value transparency and the free flow of information may target entities that restrict access to information, engaging in actions such as data leaks or distributed denial of service (DDoS) attacks to make a point about the importance of open information.

2. **Hacktivist Motivations:**

- **Protest and Activism:** Many hacktivists are motivated by the desire to protest against perceived wrongdoings or advocate for social or political change. They use hacking as a form of digital civil disobedience.

- **Whistleblowing:** Some hacktivists aim to expose wrongdoing or corruption by releasing confidential or sensitive information to the public. Their actions may be driven by a sense of moral responsibility.

- **Solidarity:** Hacktivists often seek to show solidarity with other activists or individuals who have been oppressed or persecuted. They use hacking to amplify the voices of marginalized groups.

- **Awareness and Education:** Some hacktivists target institutions to raise awareness and educate the public about issues they consider important. Their actions are aimed at sparking dialogue and change.

- **Anonymous and Decentralized Activism:** Hacktivist collectives like Anonymous operate on principles of anonymity and decentralization, allowing anyone to join their actions without needing to reveal their identity or affiliations.

It's important to note that hacktivism, while driven by ideological motivations, can sometimes cross into illegal activities, leading to legal consequences for those involved. The ethics and legality of hacktivism are subjects of debate, and hacktivist actions often exist in a legal gray area.

CHAPTER 4

Tools and Techniques of Cyber Criminals

Cybercriminals employ a wide range of tools and techniques to carry out their illegal activities in the digital realm. These tools and techniques are constantly evolving as cybercriminals adapt to technological advancements and security measures. Understanding these tools and techniques is crucial for cybersecurity professionals and law enforcement agencies to counter cyber threats effectively. Here's an overview of some common tools and techniques used by cybercriminals:

1. **Malware:**

- **Viruses:** Malicious code that attaches itself to legitimate programs and spreads when the program is executed.

- **Worms:** Self-replicating malware that spreads independently to infect other devices.

- **Trojans(or Trojan Horses):**Malware software that tricks users into unauthorized access or data legitimate allowing theft. Disguised as installing it

- **Ransomware:** Malware that encrypts a victim's files and demands a ransom for the decryption key.

- **Spyware:** Software that secretly gathers information about a user's activities and sends it to a remote attacker.

2. **Phishing:**

Cybercriminals send deceptive emails, messages, or websites to trick individuals into revealing sensitive information, such as login credentials, credit card details, or personal data.

3. **Social Engineering:**

Cybercriminals manipulate and deceive individuals into divulging confidential information or performing actions that compromise security.

4. **Distributed Denial of Service(DDoS) Attacks:**

Cybercriminals flood a network or website with excessive traffic to overwhelm it and make it unavailable to users.

5. **Password Attacks:**

Techniques like brute force attacks and dictionary attacks are used to crack. or guess passwords, gaining unauthorized access to accounts or systems.

6. **Man-in-the-Middle (MITM) Attacks:**

Cybercriminals intercept and possibly alter communications between two parties, often without their knowledge.

7. **SQL Injection:**

Attackers exploit vulnerabilities in web applications to inject malicious SQL queries, potentially gaining access to a database.

8. **Zero-Day Exploits:**

Exploiting vulnerabilities in software or hardware that are not yet known to the vendor, allowing attackers to gain unauthorized access or launch attacks before patches are available.

9. **Remote Access Tools (RATs):**

Software that allows cybercriminals to gain remote control over a victim's computer, often used for espionage, data theft, or surveillance.

10. **Botnets:**

    Networks of compromised computers or devices that are controlled by a single attacker (botmaster) and used to carry out coordinated cyberattacks, send spam, or conduct DDoS attacks.

11. **Cryptocurrency Miners:**

    Cybercriminals use victims' computer resources to mine cryptocurrencies without their knowledge, potentially slowing down the system.

12. **Keyloggers:**

    Software or hardware that records keystrokes on a victim's computer, capturing sensitive information like login credentials.

13. **Stenography:**

    Cybercriminals hide malicious code or data within seemingly innocuous files, such as images or documents.

14. **Credential Stuffing**

    Attackers use stolen usernames and passwords from one breach to gain unauthorized access to other online accounts where victims have reused the same login credentials.

15. **Dark Web Marketplaces:**

    Cybercriminals often utilize the dark web to buy and sell illegal tools, services, and stolen data, making it challenging to track their activities.

These are just a few examples of the tools and techniques employed by cybercriminals. To mitigate the risks posed by these threats, organizations and individuals should implement robust cybersecurity practices, including regular software updates, strong password policies, and user education about recognizing and avoiding common cyber threats. Law enforcement agencies and cybersecurity experts also work to identify and neutralize cybercriminal operations while continually evolving their own techniques and tools to combat cyber threats effectively.

4.1 Malware and Ransomware

Malware and ransomware are two common types of malicious software used by cybercriminals to compromise computer systems and data. Here's an explanation of each:

Malware

Malware, short for "malicious software," is a broad category of software specifically designed to harm, disrupt, or gain unauthorized access to computer systems and networks. Malware can take various forms and can be introduced into a system through infected files, links, or software downloads. Here are some common types of malwares:

1. **Viruses:** These are programs that can replicate themselves and spread to other files or systems. They often require a host file to attach to and can cause damage to the infected system.

2. **Trojans:** Trojans disguise themselves as legitimate software but contain hidden malicious code. Once installed, they can perform actions without the user's consent, such as data theft or system disruption.

3. **Worms:** Unlike viruses, worms don't need a host file. They can self-replicate and spread across networks, causing harm by overloading servers or disrupting network communication.

4. **Spyware:** Spyware is designed to collect information from a user's device, often without their knowledge or consent. It can monitor user activity, collect personal information, and relay it to a remote server.

5. **Adware:** Adware displays unwanted and often malicious advertisements to users, generating revenue for the attacker. It can slow down a computer and compromise the user's experience.

6. **Keyloggers:** Keyloggers record keystrokes on a computer, capturing sensitive information like login credentials, credit card numbers, and personal messages.

Ransomware:

Ransomware is a specific type of malware that encrypts a victim's files or locks them out of their own system. The attacker then demands a ransom, typically in cryptocurrency, in exchange for a decryption key or to restore access. Here are some key points about ransomware:

1. **Encryption:** Ransomware encrypts files on the victim's device or network, rendering them inaccessible without the decryption key.

2. **Ransom Demands:** Attackers present victims with a ransom demand, often accompanied by a timer, warning that failure to pay within a specified time will result in the permanent loss of data.

3. **Variants:** There are different types of ransomwares, including crypto ransomware (which encrypts files), locker ransomware (which locks the victim out of their system), and mobile ransomware (targeting mobile devices).

4. **Delivery Methods:** Ransomware can be delivered through various means, including malicious email attachments, compromised websites, and infected software downloads.

5. **Consequences:** Ransomware attacks can have severe consequences, including data loss, financial damage, and disruption of critical systems, especially for organizations.

6. **Prevention and Mitigation:** Preventing ransomware involves regular system backups, strong security measures, and user training. In case of an attack, it's crucial not to pay the ransom, as there's no guarantee the attacker will provide the decryption key.

Both malware and ransomware pose significant threats to individuals and organizations. Preventing and mitigating these threats require robust cybersecurity practices, including the use of antivirus software, regular system updates, user awareness, and, in the case of ransomware, strong data backup and recovery strategies.

4.2 Phishing and Social-Engineering

Phishing and Social engineering techniques used by cybercriminals to deceive individuals into divulging sensitive information, such as login credentials, personal data, or financial details. These tactics exploit human psychology and trust to manipulate victims. Here's an explanation of each:

Phishing

Phishing is a cyberattack technique that involves sending fraudulent communications, often in the form of emails, to trick individuals into taking specific actions. These actions may include clicking on malicious links, downloading malware, or disclosing personal and sensitive information. Here's how phishing works:

1. **Deceptive Communication:** Phishers create deceptive emails, messages, or websites that appear legitimate and trustworthy. They often impersonate reputable entities, such as banks, social media platforms, or government agencies.

2. **Lure:** Phishing emails contain lures designed to entice the recipient. These lures may include offers, promotions, alarming messages, or urgent requests, such as account verification or password reset.

3. **Malicious Links or Attachments:** Phishing emails typically contain links to malicious websites or attachments that, when clicked or downloaded, can install malware or direct the victim to a fake login page.

4. **Credential Theft:** Once the victim is on the fraudulent website, they are prompted to enter their login credentials or personal information, which the phisher then collects.

5. **Consequences:** Phishing can lead to unauthorized access to accounts, identity theft, financial fraud, and compromised systems.

Social Engineering:

Social engineering is a broader concept that encompasses various manipulation techniques used by cybercriminals to exploit human psychology and trust. It can include techniques like phishing, as well as others such as pretexting, baiting, and tailgating. Here's an overview of social engineering:

1. **Manipulation:** Social engineering relies on manipulating individuals or exploiting their trust, kindness, or fear to obtain sensitive information or gain unauthorized access.

2. **Pretexting:** This involves creating a fabricated scenario or pretext to obtain information from a target. For example, a social engineer might impersonate a company employee and request sensitive information from a colleague.

3. **Baiting:** Baiting uses enticing offers or fake incentives to individuals into taking specific actions, such as malware, sharing passwords, or providing confidential data. It exploits curiosity or the desire for free content.

4. **Tailgating:** In the physical world, tailgating refers to ga1n1ng unauthorized entry to a restricted area by following an authorized person. In the digital context, it can mean gaining physical access to a location or device, like a server room, through manipulation and deceit.

5. **Impersonation:** Impersonation is a common social engineering tactic where the attacker poses as someone the target trusts or respects, such as an executive, colleague, or family member.

6. **Trust Exploitation:** Social engineering exploits trust, often by posing as someone the victim knows or by using a convincing pretext to make the victim drop their guard.

Both phishing and social engineering are threats to online security and privacy. They highlight the importance of user awareness, cybersecurity training, and vigilance when dealing with unsolicited messages, requests for information, or suspicious online interactions. By recognizing and understanding these tactics, individuals and organizations can take steps to protect themselves against cyberattacks that exploit human vulnerabilities.

4.3 DDoS Attacks

A Distributed Denial of Service (DDoS) attack is a malicious and coordinated attempt to disrupt the normal functioning of a network, service, website, or online platform by overwhelming it with a flood of traffic. The goal of a DDoS attack is to make the targeted resource or service unavailable to its intended users, typically for a temporary but disruptive period.

Key characteristics and components of DDoS attacks include:

1. **Distributed Nature:** Unlike a regular DoS attack (Denial of Service), which is executed from a single source, DDoS attacks involve multiple compromised devices, often spread across the internet. These devices, known as "bots" or "zombies," are typically part of a larger network called a botnet. The attacker controls this network remotely.

2. **Traffic Overload:** DDoS attacks involve sending an overwhelming amount of traffic to the target, effectively saturating the network or server's bandwidth, processing capacity, or application resources. This excessive traffic causes a slowdown or complete unavailability of the targeted service.

3. **Variety of Attack Vectors:** DDoS attacks can employ various methods to disrupt services, including:

   - **Volumetric Attacks:** Flooding the target with a massive amount of traffic, such as a flood of data packets or requests, to consume available resources.

   - **Protocol Attacks:** Exploiting vulnerabilities in network protocols to consume resources or cause service disruptions.

   - **Application Layer:** Targeting specific applications or web servers by overwhelming them with application-level requests.

- **Amplification Attacks:** Exploiting servers or devices that amplify attack traffic, making it more potent.

4. **Motives Behind DDoS Attacks:**

   - **Financial Gain:** Competitors may launch DDoS attacks to disrupt a business, hoping to cause financial losses.

   - **Hacktivism:** Activists may employ DDoS attacks to promote a political or social cause.

   - **Extortion:** Attackers may demand a ransom to stop the stop the attack.

   - **Competitive Advantage:** Some organizations may target competitors' websites or services to gain an advantage in the market.

5. **Mitigation and Defense:**

   - Organizations often employ DDoS mitigation services, such as traffic scrubbing or rate limiting, to filter out malicious and ensure service availability.

   - Content delivery networks (CDNs) and cloud-based security services can also help protect against DDoS attacks.

   - Intrusion detection and prevention systems UDPS) can identify and block suspicious traffic patterns.

6. **Legality:** DDoS attacks are illegal in most jurisdictions, as they disrupt the operation of legitimate businesses and services. Perpetrators can face criminal charges and penalties.

7. **Botnets:** The strength of DDoS attacks relies on the size and power of the botnet. These botnets often consist of compromised devices, which may include computers, servers, routers, and IoT devices.

In summary, a DDoS attack is a disruptive cyber-attack that seeks to overwhelm a target's resources with a flood of traffic originating from multiple compromised devices. These attacks can have various motives, including financial gain and hacktivism, and they require robust defenses to mitigate their impact and ensure the continued availability of online services and resources.

CHAPTER 5
The Human Element: Cybercrime Actors

The Human Element: Cybercrime Actors" explores the individuals or groups behind cybercrimes, shedding light on the human motivations, skills, and characteristics that drive these illegal activities. Cybercrime actors, often referred to as threat actors, play a central role in the ever-evolving landscape of cyber threats. Here are the key aspects of this topic:

1. **Motivations:**

    Cybercrime actors are motivated by a range of factors, including financial gain, ideology, personal vendettas, and curiosity. Some of the primary motivations include:

    - **Financial Gain:** Many cybercriminals engage in illegal activities with the aim of making money through fraud, extortion, or theft.

    - **Hacktivism:** Some actors are driven by political or social causes, using cyberattacks to advance their ideologies or protest against governments and organizations.

    - **Espionage:** Nation-states and intelligence agencies engage in cyber espionage to gather sensitive information for national security or economic advantage.

- **Revenge or Malice:** Certain individuals use cybercrimes to seek revenge against specific targets or to cause harm for personal reasons.

- **Thrill-Seeking:** A subset of cybercriminals is motivated by the excitement and notoriety associated with hacking and cyberattacks.

2. **Skills and Expertise:**

- Cybercrime actors possess a wide range· of technical skills, including proficiency in programming, network security, exploiting software vulnerabilities. Their expertise allows to carry out sophisticated attacks and create malware.

3. **Roles and Categories:**

Cybercrime actors can be categorized into different roles and groups, each with its specific objectives and tactics. Common categories include:

- **Script Kiddies:** Novice hackers with limited technical knowledge who use pre-existing tools and scripts for simple attacks.

- **Hackers:** Skilled individuals who use their technical expertise to gain unauthorized access to systems, deface websites, or steal data.

- **Cybercriminal Organization:** Groups or networks of individuals that collaborate to commit cybercrimes, often focusing on financial fraud, identity theft, or data breaches.

- **State-Sponsored Actors:** Operatives working government agencies to conduct espionage, infrastructure, or engage in cyber warfare.on behalf of disrupt critical

- **Hacktivist Groups:** Organizations that engage in cyberattacks to advance political or social causes, often through defacement, DDoS attacks, or data leaks.

- **Insiders:** Individuals with authorized access to an organization's systems who abuse their privileges to commit cybercrimes or steal sensitive data.

- **Phishers:** Individuals or groups that engage in phishing attacks, tricking victims into revealing sensitive information or login credentials.

4. **Tools and Techniques:**

   Cybercrime actors leverage a variety of tools, malware, and techniques to carry out their activities. These may include:

   - **Malware:** Software designed to compromise systems, steal data, or enable remote access.

   - **Social Engineering:** Psychological manipulation to deceive individuals into divulging confidential information.

   - **Exploits:** Code or techniques that take advantage of vulnerabilities in software or hardware.

   - **Cryptocurrency:** The use of cryptocurrencies for - anonymous transactions and extortion payments.

5. **Geopolitical and Cross-Border Implications:**

   - The actions of cybercrime actors often transcend national borders. This complicates law enforcement efforts and requires international cooperation to combat cyber threats effectively.

Understanding the human element behind cybercrimes is crucial for devising effective cybersecurity strategies and responses. It also underscores the need for strong international cooperation and the development of legal frameworks to address cyber threats in the global context. Cybersecurity measures must consider the motivations, capabilities, and tactics of threat actors to protect individuals, organizations, and critical infrastructure from cyberattacks.

5.1 Hackers and Hacktivists

"Hackers" and "Hacktivists" are two distinct groups involved in computer-related activities, and they have different motivations and objectives.

Hackers:

1. **Definition:** Hackers are individuals who possess advanced computer and programming skills. They can manipulate computer systems, networks, and software to gain unauthorized access, find vulnerabilities, or modify code. Hackers often refer to themselves as "ethical hackers" or "white hat hackers" when they use their skills for legitimate purposes, such as testing and improving the security of systems.

2. **Motivations:**

   - **Ethical Hacking:** Some hackers are employed as cybersecurity professionals or work independently to help organizations identify and fix security weaknesses. They do so with permission and for the betterment of digital security.

   - **Malicious Intent:** Other hackers engage in illegal activities, including unauthorized data breaches, spreading malware, stealing financial information, or defacing websites. Their motivations may include financial gain, espionage, or causing damage for personal satisfaction.

3. **Types of Hackers:** ·

   - **White Hat Hackers:** Ethical hackers who work to protect systems and networks from cyber threats.

   - **Black Hat Hackers:** Criminal hackers who engage 1n unauthorized, often malicious activities.

   - **Grey Hat Hackers:** A gray area between ethical and malicious hacking, as they may expose vulnerabilities without permission but not necessarily for harmful purposes.

- **Script Kiddies:** Individuals with limited technical skills who use pre-written scripts and tools to conduct cyber-attacks.

4. **Skills and Tools:** Hackers possess a wide range of skills and use various tools to identify vulnerabilities, exploit weaknesses, and manipulate computer systems. They may use techniques like penetration testing and employ programming languages like Python or scripting languages for their activities.

Hacktivists:

1. **Definition:** Hacktivists are individuals or groups who use hacking techniques and digital platforms to promote a political, social, or ideological agenda. They often aim to raise awareness, advocate for change, or protest against perceived injustices.

2. **Motivations:**

   - **Social and Political Causes:** Hacktivists engage in cyber activities to further causes such as human rights, freedom of speech, environmental issues, or political activism.

   - **Anonymous and Disruptive Actions:** Their actions may include defacing websites, releasing confidential documents, or conducting distributed denial of service (DDoS) attacks as forms of protest.

3. **Notable Examples:**

   - **Anonymous:** A loosely organized hacktivist group known for its cyber-activism, often involving DDoS attacks and high-profile data breaches.

   - **WikiLeaks:** Whil not exclusively a hacktivist group, it has been involved in publishing confidential government and corporate documents, aiming to promote transparency and government accountability.

4. **Legal Implications:** Hacktivism can blur the line between lawful protest and illegal activity, and hacktivists often face legal consequences for their actions.

In summary, hackers are individuals with advanced computer skills who may use their abilities for various purposes, including both ethical and malicious activities. In contrast, hacktivists are motivated by social or political causes and employ hacking techniques to advance their agendas, often raising questions about the legality and ethics of their actions. Both groups play significant roles in the evolving landscape of digital security and activism.

5.2 Organized Crime Groups

Organized crime groups, often referred to as criminal organizations or criminal syndicates, are associations of individuals who engage in illegal activities for the primary purpose of generating financial gain and exerting control over various criminal enterprises. These groups are typically characterized by a structured hierarchy, a division of labor, and a persistent, long-term presence in criminal activities. Understanding organized crime groups involves examining their structure, activities, and their impact on society. Here are key points to explain this topic:

1. **Structure:**

   - Organized crime groups often have a hierarchical structure with leaders at the top who make strategic decisions, followed by various tiers of members, each with specific roles and responsibilities.

   - The structure may include positions such as underboss, consigliere, capos (captains), The boss, soldiers, and depending on the group's size and complexity.

2. **Illegal Activities:**

   These groups engage in a wide range of illegal activities, which may include:

   - **Drug Trafficking:** The distribution and sale of illicit drugs.

   - **Racketeering:** Running illegal businesses, such as gambling, prostitution, loan sharking, and extortion.

   - **Money Laundering:** Concealing the ong1ns of illegally obtained funds to make them appear legitimate.

   - **Human Trafficking:** The illegal trade of people, often for purposes of forced labor or sexual exploitation.

- **Arms Smuggling:** Illegally trading firearms or other weapons.

- **Cybercrime:** Engaging in computer-related crimes, such as hacking, online fraud, and identity theft.

- **Violent Crimes:** Organized crime groups may resort to violence, including murder, to protect their interests and territory.

3. Global Reach:

- Organized crime groups frequently operate on a global scale, participating in cross-border criminal activities.

- They may establish connections with other criminal organizations, making it challenging for law enforcement agencies to combat their activities effectively.

4. Economic Impact:

The illegal activities of organized crime groups can have a significant economic impact, leading to financial losses, increased law enforcement costs, and damage to legitimate businesses and industries.

5. Corruption and Influence:

- Organized crime groups may seek to corrupt public officials, law enforcement, and other key figures to protect their interests and avoid legal consequences.

- They often exert influence on political, economic, and social systems, which can lead to a weakened rule of law and an erosion of public trust.

6. Countermeasures:

Governments and law enforcement agencies around the world employ various countermeasures to combat organized crime. These include legislation, task forces, intelligence sharing, and international cooperation.

7. **Criminal Codes:**

   Many countries have specific criminal laws and statutes targeting organized crime, such as the Racketeer Influenced and Corrupt Organizations Act (RICO) in the United States.

8. **Criminal Enterprises:**

   Organized crime groups adapt to changing environments and opportunities. They may diversify their criminal enterprises and adapt to new technologies to maximize profits and minimize risk.

9. **History and Evolution:**

   Organized crime has a long history and has evolved over time, with different groups emerging in response to changing circumstances and markets.

Understanding organized crime groups is essential for combating their illegal activities and protecting society from the economic, social, and security threats they pose. Law enforcement efforts, along with international collaboration, play a critical role 1n addressing the challenges posed by these criminal organizations.

5.3 Insider Threats

"Insider threats refer to security risks or breaches that originate from individuals within an organization, such as employees, contractors, or business partners, who have access to the organization's systems, data, or facilities. These individuals may exploit their trusted status to intentionally or inadvertently compromise the organization's security, privacy,' or data integrity. Insider threats are a significant concern for businesses and government agencies and can take various forms, including:

1. **Malicious Insider Threats:**

   These individuals deliberately misuse their access privileges to harm the organization. Their motives may include financial gain, revenge, ideological beliefs, or personal satisfaction. Examples of malicious insider actions include data theft, fraud, sabotage, or sharing confidential information with competitors.

2. **Negligent Insider Threats:**

   These insiders don't have malicious intent but create security risks through careless or uninformed actions. Negligent insiders may accidentally expose sensitive data, fall victim to phishing attacks, or violate security policies without realizing the consequences.

3. **Compromised Insider Threats:**

   Sometimes, insiders become unwitting threats when their accounts are compromised by external actors, such as hackers or cybercriminals. Once the outsider gains control of an insider's credentials, they can exploit the trust associated with the account to carry out malicious activities.

4. **Third-Party Insider Threats:**

   Third-party contractors, suppliers, or business partners who have access to an organization's systems and data can pose insider threats. They might misuse their privileges for financial gain or inadvertently expose data through security vulnerabilities in their own systems.

5. **Espionage Insider Threats:**

Insiders with access to sensitive information may be coerced or recruited by external entities, including foreign governments, to spy on their organization or share classified data. This form of insider threat is particularly concerning for government agencies and organizations with valuable intellectual property.

Key Characteristics of. Insider Threats:

- **Access and Trust:** Insiders have legitimate access to an organization's systems and data, which ·makes them more challenging to detect because they are often trusted by default.

- **User Behavior Monitoring:** Implement user and entity behavior analytics (UEBA) solutions to detect abnormal or suspicious behavior patterns.

- **Security Awareness Training:** Train employees and contractors on security best practices, emphasizing the risks and consequences of insider threats.

- **Data Loss Prevention (DLP):** Employ DLP solutions to monitor and prevent sensitive data from leaving the organization's network.

- **Incident Response Plans:** Develop and rehearse incident response plans to address insider threat incidents promptly.

- **Regular Audits:** Conduct regular security audits to identify and mitigate vulnerabilities that could be exploited by insiders.

- **Whistleblower Programs:** Establish mechanisms for employees to report susp1c1ous behavior while protecting them from retaliation.

- **Background Checks:** Conduct thorough background checks on employees, particularly those with access to sensitive information.

In summary, insider threats pose a significant risk to organizations due to their trusted status and access to sensitive data and systems. Mitigating these threats requires a combination of technical, policy, and awareness measures to reduce the potential for harm and enhance security safeguards.

CHAPTER 6

Vulnerabilities in the Digital Ecosystems

"Vulnerabilities in the Digital Ecosystems" refer to weaknesses or gaps in the interconnected and technologically driven environment of digital systems, networks, and devices that can be exploited by cybercriminals or malicious actors. These vulnerabilities can lead to cybersecurity threats and pose risks to individuals, organizations, and the entire digital ecosystem. Understanding these vulnerabilities is crucial for addressing and mitigating potential cyber threats. Here are key aspects of vulnerabilities in the digital ecosystems:

1. **Software Vulnerabilities:**

   Software applications and operating systems may contain coding errors or bugs that can be exploited. These vulnerabilities can lead to cyberattacks, such as:

   - **Zero-Day Vulnerabilities:** Flaws that are not yet known to the software developer and have no available patches or fixes.

   - **Malware Exploitation:** Cybercriminals exploit software vulnerabilities to deliver malware, including viruses, worms, Trojans, and ransomware.

2. Weak Authentication and Passwords:

Weak or easily guessable passwords, as well as lax authentication processes, are common vulnerabilities. They can lead to unauthorized access, data breaches, and account hijacking.

3. Unpatched Systems:

Failure to apply security patches and updates leaves systems and software exposed to known vulnerabilities. Attackers actively target systems with outdated software./

4. Social Engineering:

Human factors can introduce vulnerabilities. Cybercriminals may use social engineering techniques to manipulate individuals into revealing sensitive information or taking certain actions, such as clicking on malicious links.

5. Internet of Things (loT) Vulnerabilities:

IoT devices can have weak updated regularly, making Vulnerabilities in IoT devices physical harm.security features and are often not susceptible to exploitation. can lead to privacy breaches or even

6. Inadequate Security Measures:

Organizations and individuals may not· implement proper security measures, such as firewalls, intrusion detection systems, or encryption, making their systems more vulnerable to cyberattacks.

7. Third-Party and Supply Chain Risks:

Vulnerabilities can be introduced through third-party services and components. Supply chain attacks may compromise software or hardware components before they even reach the end-user.

8. **Insider Threats:**

   Insiders with access to sensitive information may pose vulnerabilities if they misuse their privileges or engage in malicious activities. This includes employees, contractors, or business partners.

9. **Lack of Data Encryption:**

   Failing to encrypt data during storage and transmission can expose sensitive information to interception and unauthorized access.

10. **Lack of Cybersecurity Awareness:**

    A lack of cybersecurity awareness among individuals and employees can lead to vulnerabilities due to risky online behavior or insufficient knowledge of potential threats.

11. **Misconfigured Cloud Services:**

    Cloud services offer convenience but can also introduce vulnerabilities when not configured securely. Misconfigured cloud settings can expose sensitive data to the public internet.

12. **Regulatory and Compliance Gaps:**

    Failure to adhere to cybersecurity regulations and compliance standards can create vulnerabilities, potentially resulting in legal consequences or data breaches.

Addressing vulnerabilities in the digital ecosystems requires a multi faceted approach that includes proactive cybersecurity measures, regular software updates, employee training, and ongoing risk assessment. As technology evolves, new vulnerabilities may emerge, making cybersecurity an ongoing and ever-adapting challenge in the digital age.

6.1 Weakness in Digital Infrastructure

Weaknesses in digital infrastructure refer to vulnerabilities, shortcomings, or inadequacies within the technological systems and networks that make up the digital backbone of a country or organization. These weaknesses can have a detrimental impact on the functionality, security, and reliability of digital infrastructure. Here are some key aspects to consider when discussing weaknesses in digital infrastructure:

1. **Security Vulnerabilities:**

   Digital infrastructure is susceptible to security breaches, cyberattacks, and data breaches. Weaknesses in security measures, such as inadequate firewalls, outdated software, or insufficient encryption, can leave systems vulnerable to unauthorized access and data theft.

2. **Outdated Technology:**

   Aging or obsolete technology can be a significant weakness in digital infrastructure. Outdated hardware and software may lack the latest security patches, features, and capabilities required to support modern digital operations.

3. **Lack of Redundancy:**

   Redundancy is essential to ensure uninterrupted digital services. Weaknesses in redundancy, such as single points of failure, can result in downtime, data loss, and disruptions during outages.

4. **Insufficient Bandwidth:**

   Inadequate network bandwidth can lead to slow data transfer speeds, network congestion, and poor performance.

   This can be a weakness in digital infrastructure, particularly when dealing with high data traffic or bandwidth-intensive applications.

5. **Data Storage Limitations:**

   Weaknesses in data storage capacity can lead to issues such as insufficient storage for expanding datasets, causing delays or the loss of critical information.

6. **Inadequate Disaster Recovery Plans:**

   A lack of comprehensive disaster recovery plans can be a significant weakness. Without proper strategies and resources in place, digital infrastructure may not be able to recover from disasters, whether natural or cyber-related.

7. **Regulatory and Compliance Gaps:**

   Failing to meet regulatory requirements and compliance standards can weaken digital infrastructure, leading to legal and financial consequences.

8. **Humar Error:**

   Weaknesses may result from human error, such as misconfigurations, poor password management, or lack of employee training in cybersecurity best practices.

9. **Vendor Dependency:**

   Overreliance on a single technology vendor or service provider can create vulnerabilities. If that vendor experiences issues or security breaches, it can affect the entire digital infrastructure.

10. **Supply Chain Vulnerabilities:**

    Weaknesses can arise due to vulnerabilities in the supply chain, such as compromised hardware or software components that are integrated into the infrastructure.

11. **Resource Constraints:**

    Limited financial, human, or technological resources can weaken digital infrastructure. Insufficient funding or staffing may lead to suboptimal cybersecurity practices and technology investments.

12. **Scalability Challenges:**

Digital infrastructure must be able to scale to meet growing demands. Weaknesses can result 1n · performance bottlenecks during periods of increased usage.

Understanding and addressing these weaknesses 1n digital infrastructure is essential for organizations and governments to maintain the reliability, security, and efficiency of digital services and systems. Comprehensive cybersecurity measures, regular system updates, disaster recovery planning, and investment in modern technology are among the strategies used to mitigate these weaknesses and ensure a robust digital infrastructure.

6.2 Weak Cybersecurity Measures

"Weak cybersecurity measures" refer to inadequate or insufficient security practices, policies, and technologies put in place to protect digital systems, networks, and data from cyber threats. When organizations, individuals, or governments have weak cybersecurity measures, they are more vulnerable to various cyberattacks and data breaches. Here are some key aspects to understand about weak cybersecurity measures:

1. **Insufficient Protection:** Weak cybersecurity measures often mean that the digital infrastructure is inadequately protected. This may include outdated or poorly configured security software, firewalls, and intrusion detection systems.

2. **Outdated Software and Systems:** Failing to keep software, operating systems, and hardware up to date with security patches and updates can create vulnerabilities that cybercriminals can exploit.

3. **Inadequate Password and Access Controls:** -Weak cybersecurity often involves the use of weak or default passwords, lack of multi factor authentication (MFA), and inadequate user access controls. This makes it easier for unauthorized users to gain access.

4. **Poor Security Policies:** Organizations with weak cybersecurity may lack clear security policies and guidelines for employees. This can lead to risky behavior, such as sharing sensitive information over unsecured channels.

5. **Lack of Employee Training:** Employees are often the weakest link in cybersecurity. Inadequate training and awareness programs can result in mistakes and unintentional security breaches.

6. **Insufficient Data Encryption:** Weak cybersecurity measures may neglect the use of encryption for data both at rest and in transit, making it easier for attackers to intercept and exploit sensitive information.

7. **Inadequate Incident Response:** A weak incident response plan can result in delayed detection and response to cyber threats, giving attackers more time to compromise systems and steal data.

8. **Ineffective Patch Management:** Failing to promptly apply security patches and updates can leave systems exposed to known vulnerabilities that attackers can target.

9. **Ignoring Mobile Security:** With the increasing use of mobile devices, neglecting mobile security can be a weakness 1n an organization's cybersecurity posture.

10. **Underestimating Social Engineering:** Weak cybersecurity may downplay the risks of social engineering attacks, where cybercriminals manipulate individuals to divulge confidential information or perform actions that compromise security.

11. **Lack of Data Backup and Recovery:** Failing to regularly back up data and establish recovery plans can result in data loss in the event of a cyber incident.

12. **Inadequate Network Monitoring:** A lack of comprehensive network monitoring can make it difficult to detect unusual or suspicious network activities, allowing threats to go undetected.

Weak cybersecurity measures can have severe consequences, including data breaches, financial losses, damage to an organization's reputation, and legal or regulatory penalties. To strengthen cybersecurity measures, organizations and individuals should invest in up-to-date security technologies, implement robust security policies and practices, conduct regular security audits and risk assessments, and prioritize cybersecurity awareness and training. Additionally, staying informed about evolving cyber threats and best practices for cybersecurity is crucial in the digital age.

6.3 Role of Education and Awareness

The role of education and awareness is crucial in a wide range of contexts, from individual well-being to societal development. In the context of cybersecurity and digital literacy, education and awareness play a vital role in mitigating cyber threats and promoting responsible digital behavior. Here's an explanation of their significance:

1. **Cybersecurity:**

   - **Preventing Cybercrimes:** Education and awareness programs help individuals and organizations understand common cyber threats like phishing, malware, and identity theft. By recognizing these threats, people are less likely to fall victim to cybercrimes.

   - **Safe Online Practices:** Cybersecurity education teaches safe online practices, including creating strong passwords, regularly updating software, and avoiding susp1c1ous links and attachments. These practices are essential for protecting personal and sensitive information.

   - **Data Protection:** Educating individuals about the importance of data protection and privacy helps them make informed choices about sharing personal information online. Understanding data privacy regulations and rights can empower individuals to protect their data.

2. **Digital Literacy:**

   - **Access to Information:** Digital literacy, which includes the ability to access and evaluate information online, is essential in today's information age. It enables individuals to make well informed decisions and stay updated on various topics.

   - **Online Leaming:** With the increasing use of digital platforms for education, digital literacy is crucial for students and teachers. It ensures that learners can navigate online resources effectively and critically evaluate online information.

3. **Critical Thinking:**

   - **Media Literacy:** Education and awareness programs promote media literacy, helping individuals discern between reliable and unreliable sources of information, reducing the spread of misinformation and fake news.

   - **Critical Evaluation:** Digital literacy encourages critical thinking, enabling individuals to assess the credibility of online content, question assumptions, and develop a more discerning approach to information consumption.

4. **Online Safety:**

   - **Children and Adolescents:** Education and awareness efforts help young people understand the risks associated with online activities. This includes guidance on responsible social media usage, avoiding cyberbullying, and recogn1z1ng predatory behavior.

   - **Cyberbullying Prevention:** Programs aimed at preventing and addressing cyberbullying promote a culture of respect and empathy in digital interactions.

5. **Professional Development:**

   - **Workspace Skills:** In the workplace, digital literacy is crucial. Employees need the skills to use technology efficiently, safeguard company data, and adapt to the changing digital landscape.

   - **Cybersecurity Training:** Organizations benefit from cybersecurity education and awareness programs that teach employees how to recognize and respond to cyber threats, reducing the risk of data breaches and cyberattacks.

6. **Legal and Ethical Responsibilities:**

   - **Digital Ethics:** Education and awareness emphasize the ethical use of technology. Individuals and organizations are educated about the legal and moral responsibilities associated with digital activities.

7. **Civic Engagement:**

   - **Digital Citizenship:** Promoting responsible digital citizenship through education fosters active and engaged participation in online communities.

     This includes respecting others' views and engaging in constructive dialogue.

8. **Public Policy and Advocacy:**

   - Education and awareness contribute to informed public debates on digital issues. Informed citizens can advocate for policies that. protect individual rights and security in the digital realm.

In summary, education and awareness are vital tools in addressing digital challenges, promoting responsible behavior online, and enhancing cybersecurity. These initiatives empower individuals, communities, and organizations to navigate the digital landscape effectively, safeguard sensitive information, and make informed choices that contribute to a safer, more informed, and more responsible digital society.

CHAPTER 7

Government Initiatives and Cybersecurity Policies

Government initiatives and cybersecurity policies refer to the efforts and frameworks established by governments to enhance the cybersecurity posture of a nation. As cyber threats continue to evolve, governments worldwide recognize the need to safeguard their critical infrastructure, sensitive data, and the digital well-being of citizens. Here's an overview of key aspects related to government initiatives and cybersecurity policies:

1. **National Cybersecurity Strategy:**

   - Many countries formulate a National Cybersecurity Strategy that outlines their approach to addressing cyber threats comprehensively. This strategy typically involves collaboration between government agencies, private sectors, and other stakeholders.

2. **Regulatory Frameworks and Legislation:**

   - Governments enact laws and regulations to establish a legal foundation for cybersecurity. These may include data protection laws, regulations for critical infrastructure protection, and legislation addressing specific cybercrimes.

3. **National Cybersecurity Agencies:**

- Countries often establish dedicated agencies or departments responsible for overseeing and coordinating cybersecurity efforts at the national level. These agencies may lead in policy formulation, incident response, and collaboration with other entities.

4. **Collaboration with Private Sector:**

- Effective cybersecurity requires collaboration between the public and private sectors. Governments work with businesses, industries, and critical infrastructure providers to establish best practices, share threat intelligence, and enhance collective cybersecurity defenses.

5. **International Cooperation:**

- Cyber threats often transcend national borders. Governments engage in international cooperation and information sharing to strengthen global cybersecurity efforts. This may involve bilateral agreements, participation in international forums, and collaboration with global cybersecurity organizations.

6. **Incident Response and Cyber Drills:**

- Governments establish frameworks for incident response to address and mitigate cyber incidents promptly. Cybersecurity policies often include conducting regular cyber drills and exercises to test the readiness of response teams and identify areas for improvement.

7. **Cybersecurity Awareness and Education:**

- Initiatives to raise awareness about cybersecurity among the public, businesses, and government employees are a crucial component of cybersecurity policies. Education programs may cover best practices, safe online behavior, and the identification of cyber threats.

8. **Critical Infrastructure Protection:**

   - Governments recognize the significance of protecting critical infrastructure sectors such as energy, finance, healthcare, and transportation. Cybersecurity policies outline measures to secure these sectors against cyber threats.

9. **Secure Government Networks and Systems:**

   - Governments implement measures to secure their own networks and systems. This includes deploying advanced cybersecurity technologies, conducting- regular audits, and ensuring the use of best practices for secure information management.

10. **Research and Development:**

    - Governments invest in research and development initiatives to advance cybersecurity technologies and capabilities. This includes fostering innovation, supporting cybersecurity startups, and collaborating with academic institutions.

11. **National CERTs (Computer Emergency Response Teams):**

    - Establishing national CERTs or similar entities is a common practice. These teams are responsible for coordinating responses to cybersecurity incidents, disseminating threat intelligence, and providing support to organizations in handling cyber threats.

12. **Public-Private Partnerships:**

    - Governments often engage in partnerships with private sector entities to leverage their expertise and resources in enhancing national cybersecurity. Public-private collaboration can include joint initiatives, information sharing, and collaborative research projects.

13. **Adoption of Cybersecurity Standards:**

- Governments may mandate the adoption of recognized cybersecurity standards for businesses and organizations. Compliance with these standards helps ensure a baseline level of security and resilience.

Overall, government initiatives and cybersecurity policies are dynamic and evolve to address emerging threats and challenges in the digital landscape. The goal is to create a secure and resilient cyberspace that fosters economic growth, protects national security, and safeguards the privacy and well-being of citizens.

7.1 Legal Framework and Cyber Laws

The legal framework and cyber laws refer to the set of rules, regulations, and statutes established by governments to govern and regulate activities conducted in the digital realm. As technology has advanced, legal systems have evolved to address the challenges and complexities posed by cybercrimes, data breaches, and other digital activities. Here's an overview of the legal framework and cyber laws:

1. **Creation and Purpose:**

   - The legal framework for cyberspace aims to provide a structured and regulated environment for online activities.

   - It addresses various aspects, including data protection, online transactions, intellectual property rights, cybercrimes, and individual rights in the digital domain.

2. **Information Technology (IT) Acts:**

   Many countries have enacted specific legislation known as Information Technology Acts to address issues related to electronic transactions and cybercrimes.

   Examples include the Information Technology Act, 2000, 1n India and the Computer Fraud and Abuse Act (CFAA) in the United States.

3. **Key Components of Cyber Laws:**

   - **Data Protection and Privacy Laws:** These laws define how personal and sens1t1ve information should be collected, processed, and protected. Examples include the General Data Protection Regulation (GDPR) in the European Union and the California Consumer Privacy Act (CCPA) in the United States.

   - **Cybercrime Laws:** These laws outline offenses and penalties related to cybercrimes. They cover activities such as hacking, identity theft, online fraud, and the distribution of malicious software. For example, the Computer Misuse Act in the United Kingdom and the Cybercrime Prevention Act in the Philippines.

- **Electronic Transactions Law:** These laws recognize the legal validity of electronic signatures and transactions. They provide a legal framework for conducting business online. The Uniform Electronic Transactions Act (UET-A) in the United States is an example.

- **Intellectual Property Laws:** These laws protect digital content and intellectual property in the online environment.

  They address issues like copyright infringement, trademark violations, and software piracy. The Digital Millennium Copyright Act (DMCA) in the United States is a notable example.

- **Telecommunication Laws:** These laws regulate communication

  networks, internet service providers, and the use of communication technologies. They may cover issues such as net neutrality, lawful interception, and licensing requirements.

4. **International Cooperation:**

- Cyber activities often transcend national borders, making international cooperation crucial. Treaties and agreements facilitate collaboration between countries to combat cybercrimes and address global cybersecurity challenges.

5. **Challenges and Evolving Laws:**

- The dynamic nature of technology poses challenges to lawmakers who must continuously update and revise cyber laws to keep pace with emerging threats and technologies.

- Rapid advancements 1n areas like artificial intelligence, blockchain, and the Internet of Things (IoT) present new legal challenges that require thoughtful consideration and adaptation of existing laws.

6. **Enforcements and Jurisdiction:**

- Enforcement of cyber laws can be challenging, especially when offenders operate from jurisdictions with weak legal frameworks. International collaboration is essential for effective enforcement.

- Jurisdictional issues arise when cybercrimes involve multiple countries, requiring clear legal frameworks for cooperation between legal systems.

7. **Awareness and Education:**

- Public awareness and education campaigns are essential to inform individuals, businesses, and legal professionals about their rights and responsibilities in the digital realm.

In summary, the legal framework and cyber laws play a crucial role in shaping the digital landscape, providing a legal foundation for online act1v1t1es, protecting individuals and businesses, and addressing the challenges posed by cybercrimes and emerging technologies.

7.2 National Cybersecurity Strategy

A National Cybersecurity Strategy refers to a comprehensive and coordinated set of policies, guidelines, and actions that a country adopts to secure its cyberspace from cyber threats and attacks. It is a crucial framework designed to protect national interests, critical infrastructure, sensitive information, and the overall well-being of a nation in the digital age. The strategy typically involves a combination of legal, technical, educational, and diplomatic measures to address the multifaceted challenges posed by cyber threats. Here are key components and considerations related to a National Cybersecurity Strategy:

1. **Policy and Governance:**

   - **Legal Frameworks:** Establishing and updating laws and regulations related to cybersecurity to define what constitutes a cybercrime, outline penalties, and facilitate cooperation between government agencies and the private sector.

   - **Institutional Frameworks:** Designating specific agencies or bodies responsible for implementing and overseeing cybersecurity initiatives, often involving collaboration between government, private sector, and law enforcement.

2. **Critical Infrastructure Protection:**

   - Identifying and securing critical infrastructure sectors such as energy, transportation, healthcare, finance, and telecommunications from cyber threats.

   - This involves implementing standards, regulations, and best practices to enhance resilience.

3. **Incident Response and Coordination:**

   - Developing and implementing strategies for timely and effective responses to cyber incidents. This includes establishing national-level Computer Emergency

Response Teams (CERTs) and fostering coordination among different agencies and stakeholders.

4. **International Cooperation:**

   - Collaborating with other nations, international organizations, and law enforcement agencies to address cyber threats that may transcend national borders. This involves sharing threat intelligence, promoting norms of responsible behavior 1n cyberspace, and participating in international cybersecurity dialogues.

5. **Capacity Building and Awareness:**

   - Enhancing the cybersecurity capabilities of the workforce through training and education programs. This includes creating awareness among individuals, businesses, and government entities about cyber threats and best practices for staying secure.

6. **Research and Development**

   - Investing in research and development to stay ahead of emerging cyber threats. This involves supporting innovations in cybersecurity technologies and fostering a culture of continuous improvement.

7. **Public-Private Collaboration:**

   - Facilitating collaboration between the government and the private sector to strengthen overall cybersecurity. This includes sharing threat intelligence, conducting joint exercises, and establishing partnerships to address common challenges.

8. **Encryption and Data Protection:**

   - Promoting the use of strong encryption and data protection measures to safeguard sensitive information from unauthorized access and cyber-attacks.

9. **National Cyber Exercise:**

   - Conducting regular cybersecurity exercises to test the effectiveness of response plans, improve coordination among stakeholders, and identify areas for improvement.

10. **Continuous Evaluation and Updating:**

   - Regularly evaluating the effectiveness of the strategy and making necessary updates to adapt to evolving cyber threats and technological advancements.

A well-designed National Cybersecurity Strategy is essential for mitigating the risks and consequences of cyber threats, ensuring the resilience of critical infrastructure, and promoting a secure and trustworthy digital environment for citizens and businesses. The strategy should be dynamic, reflecting the evolving nature of cyber threats and the changing landscape of technology.

7.3 Collaboration with International Agencies

Collaboration with international agencies refers to the cooperation and coordination between different countries and their respective agencies to address common issues and challenges, often in areas such as security, law enforcement, public health, environmental protection, and more. In the context of cybersecurity and combating cybercrimes, collaboration with international agencies has become crucial due to the global and interconnected nature of the digital landscape. Here are key aspects to understand regarding collaboration with international agencies 1n the context of cybersecurity:

1. **Information Sharing and Threat Intelligence:**

   - Countries collaborate to share information and threat intelligence related to cyber threats and attacks.

     This includes data on the tactics, techniques, and procedures (TTPs) employed by cybercriminals, as well as indicators of compromise and other relevant information.

2. **Joint Investigations:**

   - When cybercrimes have transnational implications, law enforcement agencies from different countries may collaborate on joint investigations. This involves sharing resources, expertise, and information to apprehend cybercriminals and dismantle criminal networks.

3. **Legal Frameworks and Extradition Agreements:**

   - Collaboration often involves establishing legal frameworks and extradition agreements between countries. These agreements facilitate the process of pursuing and prosecuting cybercriminals who may operate across borders.

4. **Capacity Building and Training:**

   - Developing and enhancing the cybersecurity capabilities of nations through training programs, workshops, and capacity building initiatives is a common aspect of collaboration. This helps ensure that countries have skilled professionals equipped to handle evolving cyber threats.

5. **International Conventions and Treaties:**

   - Participating in and adhering to international conventions and treaties related to cybersecurity and cybercrime is a way for countries to signal their commitment to global efforts. The Budapest Convention on Cybercrime is an example of an international treaty aimed at addressing cybercrimes.

6. **Global Response to Cyber Incidents:**

   - In the event of a large-scale cyber incident or attack, collaboration allows for a coordinated and rapid response. This can involve sharing technical information, mitigating the impact of the incident, and collectively addressing vulnerabilities.

7. **Coordination Against Nation-State Threats:**

   - Nation-state-sponsored cyber threats often require a collaborative response.

     Countries work together to attribute attacks, apply diplomatic pressure, and establish norms and rules of behavior in cyberspace.

8. **Interpol and Europol Involvement:**

   - Interpol <International Criminal Police Organization) and Europol (European Union Agency for Law Enforcement Cooperation) play significant roles in facilitating international collaboration on cybercrime.

They provide platforms for information exchange and coordination among law enforcement agencies.

9. **Public-Private Partnerships:**

- Collaboration extends beyond government agencies to involve the private sector. Public-private partnerships are formed to share information on cyber threats, enhance cybersecurity practices, and collectively respond to cyber incidents.

10. **Cybersecurity Forums and Conferences:**

- International forums and conferences provide opportunities for stakeholders from different countries to come together, discuss emerging threats, share best practices, and foster collaboration in addressing global cybersecurity challenges.

11. **International Organizations Initiatives:**

- Organizations like the United Nations (UN), the International Telecommunication Union (ITU), and the World Economic Forum (WEF) contribute to global discussions on cybersecurity and facilitate initiatives to address cyber threats at an international level.

Collaboration with international agencies is essential to creating a united front against cyber threats, acknowledging that cybercrimes often transcend national borders. It leverages the collective knowledge, resources, and efforts of countries to build a more resilient and secure digital environment globally.

CHAPTER 8
Law Enforcements and Cybercrime Investigations

Law enforcement and cybercrime investigations involve the efforts of authorities to prevent, detect, and prosecute criminal activities in the digital realm. As technology continues to advance, so do the methods used by cybercriminals. Law enforcement agencies worldwide face the challenge of staying ahead of cyber threats to maintain the security of individuals, businesses, and critical infrastructure. Here's an explanation of the key aspects of law enforcement and cybercrime investigations:

1. **Legal Frameworks and Legislation:**

   - Governments enact and regularly update laws to address cybercrimes. These laws provide the legal foundation for investigating and prosecuting offenses in cyberspace.

   - Examples include the Computer Fraud and Abuse Act (CFAA) in the United States and the Information Technology Act in India.

2. **Specialized Cybercrime Units:**

   - Many law enforcement agencies have established specialized units or divisions dedicated to handling cybercrimes. These units consist of trained professionals with expertise in digital forensics, computer science, and cybersecurity.

3. **Digital Forensics:**

   - Digital forensics is a crucial aspect of cybercrime investigations. Investigators use specialized tools and techniques to collect, analyze, and preserve digital evidence from electronic devices, networks, and storage media.

   - This process helps identify the ongln of cyberattacks, track down perpetrators, and build a case for prosecution.

4. **International Collaboration:**

   - Cybercrimes often transcend national borders, requlnng collaboration between law enforcement agencies from different countries. International cooperation is essential for addressing cyber threats effectively.

   - Organizations like INTERPOL and Europol facilitate information sharing and joint efforts to combat cybercrime globally.

5. **Incident Response Teams:**

   - Many law enforcement agencies have established cyber incident response teams to address and mitigate the immediate impact of cyber incidents. These teams work to contain threats, analyze the extent of the damage, and assist ln the investigation.

6. **Public-Private Partnership:**

   - Collaboration between law enforcement and private sector entltles, including technology companies and cybersecurity firms, is crucial. Sharing information about emerging threats and vulnerabilities enhances the collective ability to prevent and respond to cybercrimes.

7. **Cybersecurity Training for Law Enforcement:**

   - Training programs for law enforcement personnel are essential to keep them abreast of evolving cyber threats and investigation techniques. This includes understanding the latest trends in hacking, malware, and social engineering.

8. **Legislative Challenges:**

   • Rapid technological advancements sometimes outpace the development of legislation. Law enforcement faces challenges in adapting legal frameworks to effectively address emerging cyber threats and prosecute offenders.

9. **Handling Cross-Border Jurisdiction Issues:**

   • Investigating cybercrimes that cross international be complex due to differences 1n legal borders can systems and jurisdictional challenges.Law enforcement agencies work together to overcome these obstacles.

10. **Prevention and Awareness:**

   • Law enforcement agencies play a role in educating the public and businesses about cybersecurity best practices to prevent cybercrimes. Awareness campaigns aim to reduce the likelihood of falling victim to scams and attacks.

11. **Prosecution and Legal Proceedings:**

   • Successful investigations lead to legal proceedings. Prosecutors use the gathered evidence to build a case against cybercriminals, who may face charges ranging from unauthorized access to identity theft, fraud, and more.

In summary, law enforcement and cybercrime investigations require a multidimensional approach that combines legal frameworks, technological expertise, international collaboration, and ongoing training. Effectively addressing cyber threats involves a dynamic and adaptive response from law enforcement agencies to keep pace with the evolving nature of cybercrimes.

8.1 Challenges Faced by Law Enforcement

Law enforcement and cybercrime investigations involve the efforts of authorities to preve1:t, detect, and prosecute criminal activities in the digital realm. As technology continues to advance, so do the methods used by cybercriminals. Law enforcement agencies worldwide face the challenge of staying ahead of cyber threats to maintain the security of individuals, businesses, and critical infrastructure. Here's an explanation of the key aspects of law enforcement and cybercrime investigations:

1. **Legal Frameworks and Legislation**

   - Governments enact and regularly update laws to address cybercrimes. These laws provide the legal foundation for investigating and prosecuting offenses in cyberspace.

   - Examples include the Computer Fraud and Abuse Act (CFAA) in the United States and the Information Technology Act in India.

2. **Digital Forensics:**

   - Digital forensics is a crucial aspect of cybercrime investigations. Investigators use specialized tools and techniques to collect, analyze, and preserve digital evidence from electronic devices, networks, and storage media.

   - This process helps identify the origin of cyberattacks, track down perpetrators, and build a case for prosecution.

3. **International Collaboration:**

   - Cybercrimes often transcend national borders, requ1nng collaboration between law enforcement agencies from different countries. International cooperation is essential for addressing cyber threats effectively.

   - Organizations like INTERPOL and Europol facilitate information sharing and joint efforts to combat cybercrime globally.

4. **Incident Response Teams:**

   - Many law enforcement agencies have established cyber incident response teams to address and mitigate the immediate impact of cyber incidents. These teams work to contain threats, analyze the extent of the damage, and assist 1n the investigation.

5. **Public-private Partnerships:**

   - Collaboration between law enforcement and private sector entities, including technology companies and cybersecurity firms, is crucial. Sharing information about emerging threats and vulnerabilities enhances the collective ability to prevent and respond to cybercrimes.

6. **Cybersecurity Training for Law Enforcement:**

   - Training programs for law enforcement personnel are essential to keep them abreast of evolving cyber threats and investigation techniques. This includes understanding the latest trends in hacking, malware, and social engineering.

7. **Legislative Challenges:**

   - Rapid technological advancements sometimes outpace the development of legislation.Law enforcement faces to effectively address offenders.challenges in adapting legal frameworks emerging cyber threats and prosecute

8. **Handling Cross-Border Jurisdiction Issues:**

   - Investigating cybercrimes that cross international be complex due to differences 1n legal borders can systems and jurisdictional challenges. Law enforcement agencies work together to overcome these obstacles.

9. **Prevention and Awareness:**

   - Law enforcement agencies play a role in educating the public and businesses about cybersecurity best practices to prevent cybercrimes. Awareness campaigns aim to reduce the likelihood of falling victim to scams and attacks.

10. **Prosecution and Legal Proceedings:**

- Successful investigations lead to legal proceedings. Prosecutors use the gathered evidence to build a case against cybercriminals, who may face charges ranging from unauthorized access to identity theft, fraud, and more.

In summary, law enforcement and cybercrime investigations require a multidimensional approach that combines legal frameworks, technological expertise, international collaboration, and ongoing training. Effectively addressing cyber threats involves a dynamic and adaptive response from law enforcement agencies to keep pace with the evolving nature of cybercrimes.

8.2 Success Stories Investigations in Cybercrime

It's important to note that the term "success stories in cybercrime investigations" may seem counterintuitive, as success in this context usually means the identification, apprehension, and prosecution of cybercriminals rather than celebrating criminal activities. Nonetheless, successful cybercrime investigations often involve the collaboration of law enforcement agencies, cybersecurity experts, and sometimes private entities. Here are some examples of notable success stories in cybercrime investigations:

1. **Operation Shrouded Horizon (2014):**

   - This joint operation involved law enforcement agencies from various countries, including the FBI and Europol. It targeted the Darkode hacking forum, which was a hub for cybercriminals to buy and sell hacking tools, stolen data, and engage in various illegal activities. The operation led to the arrest of many individuals associated with the forum.

2. **Gameover Zeus Cryptolocker Takedown (2014):**

   - The U.S. Department of Justice, the FBI, and international law enforcement agencies collaborated to dismantle the Gameover Zeus botnet, a network of compromised computers used to distribute the Cryptolocker ransomware. The operation involved seizing servers, disrupting the botnet, and bringing criminal charges against the individuals responsible.

3. **Silk Road Investigation (2013):**

   - The FBI shut down the Silk Road, an online darknet marketplace known for illegal drug transactions and other criminal activities. The investigation led to the arrest of Ross Ulbricht, the alleged operator of Silk Road, and the seizure of millions of dollars in Bitcoin.

4. **WannaCry Ransomware Attribution (2017):**

   - While the actual perpetrators behind the WannaCry ransomware attack remain unidentified, cybersecurity researchers and law enforcement agencies successfully traced the attack to North Korea. The attribution provided insights into state-sponsored cybercrime activities.

5. **NotPetya Attribution (2018):**

   - The NotPetya ransomware attack, which caused widespread damage globally, was attributed to the Russian military by various governments and cybersecurity experts. The attribution helped raise awareness about the use of cyber tools as part of state-sponsored activities.

6. **Operation Bayonet (2017):**

   - This international operation involved the takedown of the AlphaBay darknet marketplace, one of the largest illegal marketplaces for drugs, hacking tools, and other illicit goods. The operation involved law enforcement agencies from the U.S., Canada, and Europe.

7. **Emotet Takedown (2021):**

   - Law enforcement agencies from multiple countries collaborated to dismantle the Emotet botnet, which was a major distributor of malware used for various cybercrimes, including ransomware attacks. The operation involved seizing control of servers and infrastructure used by the botnet.

8. **FIN7 (Carbanak) Arrests (2018-19):**

   - The U.S. Department of Justice, along with international partners, arrested several key members of the cybercrime group FIN7 (also known as Carbanak). FIN7 was responsible for large scale financial theft through phishing attacks targeting businesses and financial institutions.

These success stories highlight the importance of international collaboration, public-private partnerships, and advancements in cybersecurity technologies in combating cybercrime. While challenges persist, these investigations demonstrate that coordinated efforts can lead to the identification and. prosecution of cybercriminals, contributing to a safer online environment.

8.3 Building a Cyber-Resilient Nation

Building a cyber-resilient nation refers to the strategic efforts and initiatives undertaken by a country to enhance its capability to withstand, respond to, and recover from cyber threats and attacks effectively. In an increasingly interconnected and digitized world, the resilience of a nation's critical infrastructure, government systems, businesses, and individuals against cyber threats is crucial. Here are key components and strategies involved in building a cyber-resilient nation:

1. **National Cybersecurity Strategy:**

   - Developing a comprehensive national cybersecurity strategy that outlines the objectives, priorities, and action plans to enhance cyber resilience. This involves collaboration between government agencies, private sector entities, and other stakeholders.

2. **Cybersecurity Legislation and Regulation:**

   - Establishing and enforcing cybersecurity laws and regulations to ensure that organizations follow best practices in securing their digital assets. This may include data protection laws, incident reporting requirements, and penalties for non-compliance.

3. **Collaboration and Information Sharing:**

   - Encouraging collaboration and information sharing between government agencies, private sector organizations, and international partners. Timely sharing of threat intelligence can help in proactively identifying and mitigating cyber threats.

4. **Cybersecurity Awareness and Education:**

   - Investing in cybersecurity awareness and education programs to enhance the knowledge and skills of individuals, businesses, and government employees. Educated and aware users are crucial for preventing social engineering attacks and practicing good cyber hygiene.

5. **Capacity Building and Skill Development:**

- Building a skilled cybersecurity workforce , by investing in training and education programs.

   This includes initiatives to develop a pipeline of cybersecurity professionals equipped to handle evolving threats.

6. **Secure Critical Infrastructure:**

- Implementing robust cybersecurity measures to protect critical infrastructure sectors, such as energy, healthcare, finance, and transportation. This involves adopting best practices for securing industrial control systems UCS) and supervisory control and data acquisition (SCADA) systems.

7. **Incident Response and Recovery Planning:**

- Developing and regularly testing incident response and recovery plans to ensure a swift and coordinated response to cyber incidents. This includes establishing communication protocols, defining roles and responsibilities, and conducting drills.

8. **Continuous Monitoring and Threat Intelligence:**

- Implementing continuous monitoring systems to detect and respond to cyber threats 1n real-time. Utilizing threat intelligence feeds and analytics to stay informed about the latest cyber threats and vulnerabilities.

9. **National Cyber Exercise Programs:**

- Conducting regular national cyber exercise programs to simulate cyber-attack scenarios and test the effectiveness of response and recovery mechanisms. This helps identify areas for improvement and enhances overall preparedness.

10. **Public-Private Partnerships:**

    - Establishing strong partnerships between the government and private sector entities to collectively address cyber threats. Public-private collaboration is vital for sharing resources, expertise, and intelligence.

11. **International Cooperation:**

    - Engaging in international cooperation and collaboration on cybersecurity issues. Participating in global initiatives, information-sharing forms, and collaborative efforts to combat cybercrime and promote a secure cyberspace.

12. **Research and Development:**

    - Investing in research and development to stay ahead of emerging cyber threats. This includes supporting innovation 1n cybersecurity technologies, tools, and methodologies.

Building a cyber-resilient nation is an ongoing and dynamic process that requires a multi-faceted approach involving policy, technology, education, and collaboration. The goal is to create a robust cybersecurity posture that can adapt to evolving threats and m1n1m1ze the impact of cyber incidents on a nation's security, economy, and societal well-being.

CHAPTER 9

Protecting Yourself in the Digital World

Protecting yourself in the digital world is crucial as we increasingly rely on digital technology for communication, financial transactions, and various aspects of our daily lives. The digital world presents both opportunities and risks, and taking proactive steps to safeguard your digital presence is essential. Here are key measures to help protect yourself in the digital realm:

1. **Strong and Unique Passwords:**

   - Use strong, unique passwords for each of your accounts.

   - Avoid using easily guessable information such as birthdays or names.

   - Consider using a passphrase or a combination of letters, numbers, and symbols.

2. **Two-Factor Authentication(2FA):**

   - Enable two-factor authentication whenever possible.

   - This adds an extra layer of security by requiring a second verification step, such as a code sent to your mobile device.

3. **Regular Software Updates:**

   - Keep your operating system, software applications, and antivirus programs up to date.

   - Regular updates often include security patches that protect against known vulnerabilities.

4. **Secure Wi-Fi Network:**

   - Use a strong and unique password for your Wi-Fi network to prevent unauthorized access.

   - Enable WPA3 encryption if available for enhanced security.

5. **Be Cautious with Email and Links:**

   - Avoid clicking on links or downloading , attachments from unknown or suspicious emails.

   - Verify the legitimacy of emails, especially those requesting sensitive information or financial transactions.

6. **Use Secure Websites:**

   - Look for "https://" in the URL when visiting websites, indicating a secure and encrypted connection.

   - Avoid entering sensitive information on non-secure websites.

7. **Social Media Privacy Settings:**

   - Review and adjust your privacy settings on social media platforms to control who can see your personal information.

   - Be mindful of the information you share publicly.

8. **Regularly Monitor Financial Statements:**

   - Regularly review your bank and credit card statements for any unauthorized transactions.

- Report any suspicious activity to your financial institution immediately.

9. **Backup Your Data:**

   - Regularly back up important files and data to an external drive or a secure cloud service.

   - In the event of data loss or ransomware, having backups ensures you can recover your information.

10. **Educate Yourself About Scams:**

    - Stay informed about common online scams and phishing techniques.

    - Be skeptical of unsolicited emails, messages, or phone calls asking for personal or financial information.

11. **Secure Your Mobile Devices:**

    - Use passcodes or biometric authentication (fingerprint, facial recognition) to secure your smartphones and tablets.

    - Install security updates and use reputable antivirus apps on mobile devices.

12. **Monitor Your Online Presence:**

    - Regularly check your online accounts for any unusual activity.

    - Set up alerts for account logins or changes to account settings.

13. **Educate Yourself on Digital Literacy:**

    - Stay informed about digital security best practices.

    - Understand the risks associated with sharing personal information online.

14. **Secure Your Home Network:**

    - Change default router passwords and use strong encryption.

- Consider setting up a separate guest network for visitors.

15. Regularly Review App Permissions:

- Periodically review and adjust the permissions granted to mobile apps.

- Be cautious about apps that request excessive access to your personal information.

By adopting these practices, you can significantly enhance your digital security and reduce the risk of falling victim to cyber threats. Being vigilant and proactive in protecting your digital presence is essential in today's interconnected world.

9.1 Personal Cyber Hygiene

"Personal cyber hygiene" refers to the practices and habits individuals adopt to maintain a secure and healthy digital presence. In the context of cybersecurity, it involves taking proactive measures to protect personal information, devices, and online accounts from various cyber threats. Practicing good personal cyber hygiene is crucial in today's digital age, where individuals are connected to the internet and digital devices on a daily basis. Here are key components of personal cyber hygiene:

1. **Strong Passwords:**

   - Use complex passwords that include a mix of upper and lower case letters, numbers, and special characters.

   - Avoid using easily guessable information, such as birthdays or common words.

   - Regularly update passwords and avoid using the same password across multiple accounts.

2. **Multi-Factor Authentication (MFA):**

   - Enable MFA whenever possible to add an extra layer of security to your accounts.

   - MFA requires users to provide two or more verification factors, typically something they know (password) and something they have (authentication code on a device).

3. **Regular Software Updates:**

   - Keep operating systems, software applications, and antivirus programs up to date.

   - Software updates often include security patches that address vulnerabilities and protect against known threats.

4. **Awareness and Education:**

   - Stay informed about common cyber threats, phishing tactics, and social engineering attacks.

- Regularly educate yourself about cybersecurity best practices and share this knowledge with others, especially within your household.

5. **Secure Wi-Fi Networks:**

   - Use strong encryption (e.g., WPA3) for your home Wi-Fi network.

   - Change default router login credentials arid regularly update the Wi-Fi password.

6. **Safe Browsing Practices:**

   - Be cautious when clicking on links, especially in emails or messages from unknown sources.

   - Verify the legitimacy of websites before providing personal information or making online transactions.

7. **Data Backup:**

   - Regularly back up important data to an external hard drive or cloud storage.

   - In case of data loss due to cyber incidents, having backups ensures that you can recover essential information.

8. **Privacy Settings:**

   - Review and adjust privacy settings on social media platforms and other online accounts.

   - Limit the amount of personal information shared publicly.

9. **Email Security:**

   - Be cautious about email attachments and links, especially from unknown or unexpected sources.

   - Use email filtering tools to detect and filter out potential phishing emails.

10. **Device Security:**

    - Use a reputable antivirus or anti-malware program on all devices, including computers, smartphones, and tablets.

    - Implement device encryption to protect sensitive data in case of theft or loss.

11. **Regular Security Audits:**

    - Periodically review and audit your online accounts, checking for any suspicious activities or unauthorized access.

    - Close or deactivate accounts that are no longer in use.

12. **Secure Online Transactions:**

    - Use secure and reputable websites for online transactions.

    - Avoid making financial transactions over public Wi-Fi networks, especially for sensitive transactions like online banking.

By incorporating these practices into their digital routines, individuals can significantly enhance their personal cyber hygiene, reducing the risk of falling victim to cyber threats and maintaining a more secure online presence.

CHAPTER 10
Future Trends and Challenges

The exploration of future trends and challenges is crucial for anticipating and adapting to the rapidly evolving landscape of technology, society, and various industries. This analysis involves forecasting the likely trajectories of advancements, innovations, and disruptions while also identifying potential obstacles and difficulties. Here's an overview of the topic "future trends and challenges" across different domains:

Future Trends:

1. **Technology Advancements:**

    - **Artificial Intelligence (AL) and Machine Learning (ML):** Continued integration of AI and ML into various applications, from autonomous systems to personalized services.

    - **Quantum Computing:** Advancements in quantum computing could revolutionize data processing, cryptography, and problem-solving.

    - **SG Technology:** Widespread adoption of 5G networks, enabling faster and more reliable wireless communication.

2. **Biotechnology and Healthcare:**

- **Precision Medicine:** Tailoring medical treatments based on individual genetic profiles.

- **Gene Editing:** Advancements in CRISPR and other gene-editing technologies for therapeutic applications.

- **Telemedicine:** Growing reliance on remote healthcare services and telemedicine platforms.

3. **Climate and Sustainability:**

- **Renewable Energy:** Increased reliance on renewable energy Sources and technological innovations to address climate change.

- **Circular Economy:** Emphasis on sustainable practices, resource efficiency, and waste reduction.

4. **Digital Transformation:**

- **Internet of Things(IoT):** Expansion of IoT applications in smart cities, agriculture, healthcare, and manufacturing.

- **Blockchain Technology:** Continued exploration of blockchain for secure and transparent transactions beyond cryptocurrencies.

5. **Cybersecurity:**

- **AI-Driven Cybersecurity:** Leveraging AI to enhance threat detection and response capabilities.

- **Zero Trust Security Models:** A shift toward continuous verification and authorization rather than trusting entities based on location.

6. **Education and Remote Work:**

- **Hybrid Work Models:** A blend of remote and in-person work environments.

- **Online Education:** Evolution of online learning platforms and the integration of virtual reality (VR) and augmented reality (AR) in education.

Challenges:

1. **Cybersecurity Threats:**

   - **Sophisticated Attacks:** The rise of more advanced and complex cyber threats.

   - **Supply Chain Vulnerabilities:** Increased risks associated with supply chain attacks.

2. **Ethical Considerations:**

   - **AI Bias and Ethics:** Addressing bias in AI algorithms and ensuring ethical use of emerging technologies.

   - **Privacy Concerns:** Balancing technological advancements with individual privacy rights.

3. **Environmental Impact:**

   - **E-Waste:** The environmental impact of electronic waste generated by the rapid turnover of technology.

   - **Energy Consumption:** Balancing the demand for technology with the need to reduce energy consumption.

4. **Public Health Preparedness:**

   - **Global Health Crises:** Preparing for and responding to future pandemics and global health emergencies.

   - **Vaccine Distribution:** Ensuring equitable and efficient distribution of vaccines and medical resources.

5. **Digital Inclusion:**

   - **Digital Divide:** Addressing disparities in digital access and skills across different populations.

   - **Accessibility:** Ensuring technology is accessible to people with disabilities.

6. **Regulatory and Legal Frameworks:**

   - **Data Governance:** Establishing effective frameworks for data governance and protection.

   - **Regulation of Emerging Technologies:** Developing regulations that balance innovation with public safety and ethical considerations.

7. **Geopolitical Tensions:**

   - **Technological Sovereignty:** Navigating tensions related to technology ownership, data control, and international collaboration.

   - **Trade and Technology Wars:** Managing the impact of trade conflicts on the global technology landscape.

Anticipating these future trends and challenges requires ongoing collaboration, research, and adaptability across various sectors. It's essential for policymakers, businesses, and individuals to stay informed and proactive in navigating the complexities of an ever evolving technological and societal landscape.

10.1 Emerging Threats

Emerging threats in the context of cybersecurity refer to new or evolving risks and challenges that pose potential harm to individuals, organizations, and information systems. These threats often arise due to advancements in technology, changes in cybercriminal tactics, or vulnerabilities in existing systems. Staying informed about emerging threats is crucial for developing effective cybersecurity strategies. Here are some key categories of emerging threats:

1. **Advanced Persistent Threats (APTs):**

   - APTs are sophisticated and targeted cyberattacks typically orchestrated by well-funded and organized threat actors, such as nation-states or advanced cybercriminal groups. APTs aim to gain unauthorized access to networks and remain undetected for an extended period, often for espionage or data theft.

2. **Ransomware Evolution:**

   Ransomware attacks continue to evolve, with attackers employing more advanced techniques. This includes:

   - **Double Extortion:** Threatening to release sensitive data 1n addition to encrypting it, increasing the pressure on victims to pay a ransom.

   - **Ransomware-as-a-Service (RaaS):** Cybercriminals can now rent or purchase ransomware tools and infrastructure, lowering the barrier to entry for less experienced attackers.

3. **Supply Chain Attacks:**

   - Attackers target vulnerabilities within the supply chain to compromise products or services before they reach end-users. This includes manipulating software updates, compromising hardware components, or infiltrating third-party vendors.

4. **Cloud Security Risks:**

   - As organizations increasingly migrate to cloud environments, new security challenges emerge·. These include misconfigurations, data breaches, and unauthorized access.

     to cloud resources. Shared responsibility models between cloud service providers and users add complexity to securing cloud environments.

5. **Internet of Things (IoT) Vulnerabilities:**

   - The proliferation of IoT devices introduces new attack vectors. Insecure IoT devices, lacking proper security measures, can be exploited for various purposes, including launching DDoS attacks or serving as entry points into networks.

6. **Deepfake Technology:**

   - Deepfakes involve the use of artificial intelligence to create realistic fake videos or audio recordings. Cybercriminals can use this technology for social engineering attacks, identity theft, or spreading disinformation.

7. **5G Network Security Challenges:**

   - The rollout of SG networks introduces new security considerations. While SG brings faster speeds and improved connectivity, it also presents challenges such as increased attack surfaces, potential for new types of attacks, and the need for robust encryption.

8. **Artificial Intelligence (AI) and Machine Leaming (ML) Threats:**

   - Cybercriminals are leveraging AI and ML to enhance the sophistication of attacks. This includes crafting more convincing phishing emails, automating malware creation, and evading traditional security measures.

9. **Quantum Computing Threats:**

   - The development of quantum computing poses a threat to traditional encryption methods. While quantum computers are not yet widely available, their future existence may render current cryptographic systems vulnerable.

10. **Regulatory and Compliance Risks:**

    - The evolving landscape of data protection regulations and compliance requirements introduces risks for organizations. Non-compliance may lead to legal consequences and reputational damage.

11. **Cybersecurity Workforce Shortage:**

    - The shortage of skilled cybersecurity professionals remains an ongoing challenge. This shortage hampers organizations' ability to effectively defend against and respond to cyber threats.

Staying proactive in identifying and addressing emerging threats involves continuous monitoring, threat intelligence analysis, and collaboration within the cybersecurity community. Organizations need to adapt their security measures to mitigate these evolving risks and build resilience in the face of an ever-changing threat landscape.

10.2 The Role of A.I. in Cybersecurity

The role of Artificial Intelligence (AI) in cybersecurity is increasingly vital as the cybersecurity landscape becomes more complex and dynamic. AI technologies are leveraged to enhance the detection, prevention, and response capabilities of cybersecurity systems. Here are key aspects of how AI contributes to cybersecurity:

1. **Threat Detection and Analysis:**

   - **Anomaly Detection:** AI systems analyze vast amounts of data to establish baseline behaviors, allowing them to identify anomalies that may indicate potential security threats.

   - **Behavioral Analytics:** AI monitors user and system behavior, recogn1z1ng patterns associated with malicious activities, helping in early threat detection.

2. **Incident Response:**

   - **Automated Response:** AI can facilitate automated responses to certain types of security incidents, enabling faster and more efficient reactions to threats.

   - **Orchestration and Automation:** AI-driven orchestration tools can coordinate incident response efforts, ensuring a coordinated and rapid reaction to security incidents.

3. **Malware Detection and Prevention:**

   - **Pattern Recognition:** AI algorithms can identify patterns associated with known malware, improving the detection of malicious code and files.

   - **Heuristic Analysis:** AI can perform heuristic analysis to identify new, previously unseen forms of malware based on their behavior.

4. **User Authentication and Access Control:**

   - **Biometric Authentication:** AI-based biometric systems enhance user authentication by verifying unique biological traits, such as fingerprints or facial features.

- **Behavioral Biometrics:** AI analyzes user behavior patterns to establish a baseline and detect anomalies, helping identify unauthorized access.

5. **Phishing Detection:**

- **Natural Language Processing (NLP):** AI-powered systems use NLP to analyze text and identify phishing attempts in emails or messages by recognizing patterns associated with malicious content.

6. **Network Security:**

- **Intrusion Detection and Prevention System (IDPS):** AI enhances the capabilities of IDPS to identify and respond to potential network intrusions in real-time.

- **Network Traffic Analysis:** AI analyzes network traffic patterns to identify anomalies and potential security threats.

7. **Vulnerability Management:**

- **Automated Vulnerability Assessment:** AI tools can automatically scan and assess systems for vulnerabilities, helping organizations identify and address potential weaknesses.

- **Risk Prioritization:** AI can prioritize vulnerabilities based on potential impact and the likelihood of exploitation, assisting in efficient risk management.

8. **Predictive Analysis and Threat Intelligence:**

- **Machine Learning in Threat Intelligence:** AI, especially machine learning, is used to analyze large datasets and predict emerging threats based on historical data, aiding in proactive threat mitigation.

9. **Security Analytics:**

- **Big Data Analytics:** AI handles the vast amounts of data generated by security systems, helping security analysts make sense of the information and identify relevant patterns or anomalies.

10. **Adaptive Security Measures:**

    - **Adaptive Authentication:** AI enables systems to adjust authentication requirements based on risk factors, such as the user's location, behavior, or device used.

11. **Continuous Monitoring and Leaming:**

    - **Machine Leaming Models:** AI systems continuously learn and adapt to evolving threats by updating machine learning models based on new data and emerging threat intelligence.

12. **Insider Threat Detection:**

    - **Behavioral Analysis:** AI analyzes user behavior to identify potential insider threats by recognizing deviations from normal patterns.

In summary, AI plays a crucial role in strengthening cybersecurity defenses by offering advanced threat detection, rapid response capabilities, and the ability to adapt to evolving cyber threats. As cyber threats continue to evolve, the integration of AI technologies becomes increasingly important to bolster the resilience of cybersecurity measures.

10.3 International Cooperation in Combating Cybercrimes

International cooperation in combating cybercrimes-is crucial due to the global and interconnected nature of the digital landscape. Cybercriminal activities often transcend national borders, making collaboration between countries essential to effectively prevent, investigate, and prosecute cybercrimes. Here are key aspects of international cooperation in combating cybercrimes:

1. **Information Sharing and Intelligence Exchange:**

   - Countries collaborate by sharing information related to cyber threats. This includes and intelligence details aboutcybercriminal tactics, techniques, and procedures, as well as indicators of compromise.

   - International organizations, such as INTERPOL and Europol, facilitate the exchange of cyber threat intelligence among member countries.

2. **Cross-Border Investigation:**

   - Cybercrimes often involve perpetrators located In different countries. International cooperation enables law enforcement agencies to conduct cross-border investigations.

   - Joint task forces and collaboration between cybercrime units in different countries help track down and apprehend cybercriminals.

3. **Legal Frameworks and Extradition Treaties:**

   - Establishing effective legal frameworks and extradition treaties Is essential for bringing cybercriminals to justice. These agreements enable countries to cooperate in prosecuting individuals who commit cybercrimes across borders.

- Harmonizing legal definitions and penalties for cybercrimes helps ensure consistency in addressing these offenses globally.

4. **Capacity Building and Training:**

- Developing the capacity of law enforcement agencies in different countries to combat cybercrimes is crucial, international cooperation involves providing training, sharing best practices, and improving the skills of investigators and prosecutors.

- Collaboration with international organizations and cybersecurity experts helps enhance the capabilities of nations with developing cybersecurity infrastructures.

5. **Public-Private Partnerships:**

- Collaboration between governments and the private sector is essential in combating cybercrimes. Private companies often possess valuable threat intelligence and resources that can assist in investigations.

- Information-sharing platforms, such as the Cyber Threat Alliance, facilitate collaboration between private cybersecurity firms to share intelligence and improve global cyber defenses.

6. **International Conventions and Threats:**

- Various international conventions and treaties have been established to address cybercrimes. Examples include the Budapest Convention on Cybercrime, the United Nations Convention against Transnational Organized Crime (UNTOC), and the Commonwealth Cyber Declaration.

- These agreements provide a framework for countries to cooperate on legal, technical, and policy aspects of combating cybercrimes.

7. **Joint Cybersecurity Exercises and Drills:**

   - Conducting joint cybersecurity exercises and drills helps countries test their readiness and response capabilities in the event of a large-scale cyber incident.

   - Exercises involve simulating cyberattacks and practicing coordinated responses, fostering better international cooperation and communication during real incidents.

8. **Inter-Government Organizations and Initiatives:**

   - Organizations like the United Nations (UN), the International Telecommunication Union (ITU), and regional bodies play a role in coordinating international efforts to combat cybercrimes.

   - Initiatives like the Global Forum on Cyber Expertise (GFCE) aim to promote international cooperation 1n building and enhancing cybersecurity capabilities.

9. **Diplomatic Engagement:**

   - Diplomatic channels are utilized to address cyber threats and promote responsible behavior in cyberspace. High-level dialogues and diplomatic engagements between nations help build trust and cooperation on cybersecurity issues.

10. **Norms of Responsible State Behavior in Cyberspace:**

   - The development and adherence to norms of responsible state behavior in cyberspace contribute to a more stable and secure digital environment. Nations work together to establish and promote these norms, fostering a common understanding of acceptable behavior in cyberspace.

In summary, international cooperation is indispensable in the fight against cybercrimes. The collaborative efforts of governments, law enforcement agencies, private ent1t1es, and international organizations are vital for creating a secure and resilient global cyberspace. As cyber threats continue to evolve, ongoing cooperation is essential to address the challenges posed by cybercriminals and state-sponsored actors.

CHAPTER 11

The Roads Ahead

The phrase "the roads ahead in increasing cybercrimes in India" seems to be suggesting a focus on the future challenges and potential trajectories of cybercrimes in the country. While it's essential to clarify that addressing cybercrimes is a priority, I assume you might be interested in understanding the potential future trends or challenges in this context. Here's an exploration of factors that could contribute to the evolving landscape of cybercrimes in India:

1. **Digital Transformation and Increased Connectivity:**

   - As India continues its journey of digital transformation, the increasing adoption of technology and connectivity may lead to a larger attack surface for cybercriminals. More devices, networks, and systems coming online present more opportunities for exploitation.

2. **Rapid Technological Advancements:**

   - Emerging technologies, such as artificial intelligence, the Internet of Things (IoT), and SG, offer tremendous benefits but also introduce new cyber threats. Cybercriminals are likely to exploit vulnerabilities 1n these technologies for various malicious purposes.

3. **Sophistication of Cyber Attacks:**

   - Cybercriminals are expected to become more sophisticated, using advanced tools and techniques to carry out cyberattacks. This includes more complex malware, targeted phishing campaigns, and advanced persistent threats.

4. **Financial Motives and Online Transactions:**

   - The increasing use of online financial transactions, mobile banking, and digital payment systems provides cybercriminals with lucrative targets. Financial fraud, ransomware attacks, and other financially motivated crimes may become more prevalent.

5. **Cybersecurity Skills Shortage:**

   - The demand for skilled cybersecurity professionals is likely to outstrip the supply, leading to a shortage of qualified experts. This gap can create challenges for organizations in effectively defending against cyber threats.

6. **Globalization of Cybercrime:**

   - Cybercriminal activities are not constrained by geographical borders. As cybercriminals operate globally, India may become a target for international cybercrime syndicates, and coordinated attacks with a global impact may increase.

7. **Cybersecurity Awareness and Education:**

   - While awareness about cybersecurity is increasing, there is still a need for more comprehensive education and training programs. Individuals and organizations need to be better informed about cyber threats and best practices for prevention.

8. **Regulatory and Legal Challenges:**

   - The legal and regulatory framework surrounding cybercrimes is continuously evolving. New laws and regulations are expected to be enacted, but challenges in enforcement and keeping up with the dynamic nature of cyber threats may persist.

9. **Critical Infrastructure and Vulnerabilities.**

- With the growing dependence on digital technologies in critical infrastructure sectors such as energy, healthcare, and transportation, the potential impact of cyber-attacks on essential services may increase.

10. **Social Engineering and Targeted Attacks:**

- Cybercriminals often exploit human vulnerabilities through social engineering tactics. Targeted attacks on individuals, businesses, and government entities may become more sophisticated and harder to detect.

11. **Emergence of New Threat Vectors:**

- As technologies evolve, new threat vectors arise. For example, the proliferation of IoT devices can vulnerabilities that cybercriminals might exploit unauthorized access or launch attacks. introduce to gain

Addressing the potential roads ahead in increasing cybercrimes in India requires a comprehensive approach involving technological advancements, cybersecurity policies, public awareness, international collaboration, and an agile response to emerging threats. Strengthening cybersecurity measures and investing 1n the development of skilled professionals will be crucial to mitigating the risks associated with the evolving cyber threat landscape.

11.1 Recommendation of Policy Makers

The topic "recommendations of policymakers" generally refers to the guidance or suggestions provided by government officials and policymakers to address specific issues or challenges within a given context. These recommendations often arise from thorough analysis, research, and consideration of various factors related to a particular policy area. In the context of cybersecurity or any other domain, policymakers may offer recommendations to improve existing policies, address emerging threats, or enhance overall governance. Here's an overview of how recommendations of policymakers might unfold, particularly in the realm of cybersecurity:

1. **Assessment of Current Landscape:**

   - Policymakers begin by assessing the current state of affairs within the domain under consideration, whether it's cybersecurity, healthcare, education, or any other policy area. This involves understanding existing challenges, vulnerabilities, and strengths.

2. **Identification of Key Issues:**

   - Once the assessment is complete, policymakers identify key issues or areas that require attention and improvement. In the context of cybersecurity, this could involve concerns such as data breaches, ransomware attacks, inadequate regulations, or gaps in critical infrastructure protection.

3. **Consultation and Collaboration:**

   - Policymakers often engage in consultation and collaboration with various stakeholders, including experts, industry representatives, academics, and the public. Gathering diverse perspectives helps in formulating comprehensive and effective recommendations.

4. **Policy Development and Revision:**

   - Policymakers work on developing or rev1s1ng policies based on the insights gained from the assessment and consultation processes. These policies could encompass a wide range of measures, from legislative changes and regulatory updates to the implementation of new initiatives or programs.

5. **Strategic Planning:**

   - Policymakers may provide recommendations for strategic planning, outlining a roadmap for achieving specific goals within the policy area. In the context of cybersecurity, this might involve strategies for enhancing national cybersecurity capabilities, improving incident response mechanisms, or fostering international collaboration.

6. **Resource Allocation:**

   - Policymakers consider the allocation of resources, both financial and human, to support the implementation of recommended policies. Adequate resources ·•are crucial for the effective execution of proposed measures.

7. **Public Awareness and Education:**

   - Policymakers often emphasize the importance of public awareness and education in their recommendations. This could include campaigns to educate individuals· and businesses about cybersecurity best practices, the potential risks, and ways to stay protected.

8. **Monitoring and Evaluation:**

   - Policymakers recommend mechanisms for monitoring and evaluating the effectiveness of implemented policies. Regular assessments help policymakers understand whether the intended outcomes are being achieved and if adjustments are necessary.

9. **International Cooperation:**

   - In certain policy areas, particularly those with global implications like cybersecurity, policymakers may recommend fostering international cooperation. Collaboration with other nations and organizations can enhance collective efforts to address shared challenges.

10. **Legislative and Regulatory Changes:**

    - Policymakers may recommend specific legislative or regulatory changes to address gaps or strengthen existing frameworks. This could involve introducing new laws, updating outdated regulations, or enhancing enforcement mechanisms.

11. **Incentives and Penalties:**

    - Policymakers may recommend the introduction of incentives for compliance with desired behaviors or penalties for non compliance. This approach can encourage adherence to recommended policies.

In essence, recommendations of policymakers are a critical aspect of the policy-making process, guiding the development, implementation, and evaluation of policies that aim to address complex challenges and improve societal outcomes.

11.2 Strengthening Infrastructure India's Cybersecurity

Strengthening India's cybersecurity infrastructure is a critical imperative to protect the nation's digital assets, sensitive information, and critical infrastructure from evolving cyber threats. A robust cybersecurity framework is essential for ensuring the resilience of government systems, safeguarding businesses, and protecting the privacy and security of individuals. Here are key aspects and strategies involved in strengthening India's cybersecurity infrastructure:

1. **National Cyber Security Strategy (NCSS):**

   - Developing and implementing a comprehensive Security Strategy 1s crucial. This strategy overarching v1s1on, goals, and measures cybersecurity at the national level.

2. **Regulatory Frameworks and Legislation:**

   - National Cyber outlines the to enhance Strengthening and updating existing cybersecurity laws and regulations to address emerging threats. This includes ensuring that the legal framework aligns with international best practices and facilitates effective prosecution of cybercriminals.

3. **Cybersecurity Awareness and Education:**

   - Promoting cybersecurity awareness and education programs at various levels, including schools, businesses, and government organizations. A well-informed population is better equipped to recognize and mitigate cyber threats.

4. **Public-Private Collaboration:**

   - Fostering collaboration between the government, private sector, academia, and cybersecurity experts. Public-private partnerships can enhance information sharing, joint threat intelligence, and collaborative efforts to address cybersecurity challenges.

5. **Incident Response and Cyber Crisis Management:**

   - Establishing a robust incident response framework to promptly identify, contain, and mitigate cyber incidents. This includes developing cyber crisis management plans to respond effectively to large-scale cyberattacks_.

6. **Critical Infrastructure protection:**

   - Implementing measures to protect critical infrastructure, such as power grids, financial systems, and healthcare networks, from cyber threats. This involves conducting regular cybersecurity assessments and implementing security-by-design principles.

7. **Capacity Building and Skill Development:**

   - Investing in the development of a skilled cybersecurity workforce through training programs, certifications, and academic initiatives. Building a pool of skilled professionals is crucial for managing and responding to cyber threats effectively.

8. **Continuous Monitoring and Threat Intelligence:**

   - Implementing continuous monitoring mechanisms and leveraging threat intelligence to stay ahead of evolving cyber threats. This includes utilizing advanced technologies like artificial intelligence and machine learning for real-time threat detection

9. **Secure Software Development Practices:**

   - Encouraging the adoption of secure software development practices to m1n1m1ze vulnerabilities 1n applications and systems. This includes regular security assessments and code reviews.

10. **Secure Network Architecture:**

   - Designing and implementing secure network architectures that incorporate firewalls, intrusion detection and prevention systems, secure . gateways, and encryption to protect data in transit.

11. **International Collaboration:**

   - Collaborating with international organizations, governments, and cybersecurity communities to share threat intelligence, best practices, and collaborate on global cybersecurity initiatives.

12. **Data Protection and Privacy Measures:**

   - Strengthening data protection and privacy laws to safeguard personal and sensitive information. This 1nvolves implementing measures such as data encryption, access controls, and data breach notification requirements.

13. **Emerging Technology Governance:**

   - Establishing governance frameworks for emerging technologies like artificial intelligence, blockchain, and the Internet of Things (IoT) to ensure that their deployment 1s secure and aligns with cybersecurity best practices.

14. **Regular Cybersecurity Audits and Assessments:**

   - Conducting regular cybersecurity audits and assessments to identify vulnerabilities and weaknesses. This proactive approach helps organizations address potential risks before they can be exploited.

Strengthening India's cybersecurity infrastructure is a dynamic and ongoing process that requires collaboration, continuous improvement, and adaptability to emerging threats. By adopting a multi-faceted and holistic approach, India can build a resilient cybersecurity ecosystem capable of protecting its digital assets and promoting a secure digital environment.

11.3 The Role of Business and Individual

The role of businesses and individuals in the context of cybersecurity is crucial in fostering a secure digital environment. Both entities play distinct but interconnected roles in safeguarding sensitive information, preventing cybercrimes and contributing to the overall resilience of the digital ecosystem. Here's an explanation of the roles of businesses and individuals in cybersecurity:

The Role of Businesses:

1. **Establishing a Cybersecurity Culture:** Businesses need to foster a culture of cybersecurity among their employees. This involves creating awareness, providing training, and instilling a sense of responsibility for maintaining a secure digital environment.

2. **Robust Cybersecurity Policies:** Businesses should develop and enforce comprehensive cybersecurity policies and procedures. These policies should cover areas such as data protection, access controls, incident response, and secure coding practices.

3. **Investing in Security Infrastructure:** Businesses must allocate resources to invest in advanced cybersecurity technologies and infrastructure. This includes firewalls, intrusion detection systems, antivirus software, encryption tools, and regular security audits.

4. **Securing Customer Data:** For businesses that collect and store customer data, securing this information is paramount. Compliance with data protection regulations and implementing measures to safeguard customer privacy are essential.

5. **Incident Response Planning:** Having a well-defined incident response plan is crucial. Businesses should be prepared to respond swiftly and effectively to cybersecurity incidents, minimizing the impact of potential breaches and restoring normal operations.

6. **Employee Training and Awareness:** Regular training sessions for employees on cybersecurity best practices, recognizing phishing attempts, and understanding the importance of strong password management contribute to a more resilient defense against cyber threats.

7. **Collaboration and Information Sharing:** Businesses should collaborate with industry peers, share threat intelligence, and participate in information-sharing forums. This collective approach strengthens the overall cybersecurity posture across sectors.

The Role of Individuals

1. **Practicing Good Cyber Hygiene:** Individuals must practice good cyber hygiene, including using strong, unique passwords, enabling multi-factor authentication, and keeping software and devices up to date with the latest security patches.

2. **Being Skeptical of Phishing Attempts:** Individuals should be cautious of unsolicited emails, messages, or phone calls. Recognizing and avoiding phishing attempts is crucial to preventing unauthorized access to personal information.

3. **Securing Personal Devices:** Securing personal devices, such as smartphones, tablets, and computers, is vital. This includes using security features, installing antivirus software, and regularly updating software to patch vulnerabilities.

4. **Protecting Personal Information Online:** Individuals should be mindful of the information they share online, including on social media. Limiting the exposure of personal details helps mitigate the risk of identity theft and social engineering attacks.

5. **Reporting Suspicious Activity:** Individuals should promptly report any suspicious online activity, such as phishing

attempts or unauthorized access, to the appropriate authorities or the IT department of their organization.

6. **Participating in Cybersecurity Education:** Individuals should actively engage in cybersecurity education programs provided by their employers, educational institutions, or online platforms. Staying informed about the latest cyber threats and preventive measures is essential.

7. **Supporting a Culture of Security:** Individuals play a role in promoting a culture of security within their workplaces and communities. Encouraging others to prioritize cybersecurity and follow best practices contributes to a collective effort in creating a safer digital environment.

In summary, the roles of businesses and individuals in cybersecurity are interlinked. Businesses need the active participation of employees in maintaining a secure environment, while individuals benefit from the cybersecurity measures and policies implemented by their organizations. A collective commitment to cybersecurity enhances the overall resilience of the digital landscape.

CHAPTER 12

Conclusion

In conclusion, the escalating trend of cybercrimes 1n India underscores the critical need for proactive measures to address the growing challenges in the digital landscape. As technology becomes more pervasive in daily life and across various sectors, the potential targets for cybercriminals multiply, posing significant threats to individuals, businesses, and the nation's security. The high-profile cases and diverse motives behind cybercrimes demonstrate the evolving sophistication of malicious actors and the urgency to fortify cybersecurity frameworks. To combat this rising tide of cyber threats, India must prioritize continuous improvement in cybersecurity infrastructure, enhance public awareness and digital literacy, and strengthen legal and regulatory frameworks. Collaboration between government agencies, law enforcement, businesses, and the cybersecurity community is crucial to fostering a resilient and secure digital ecosystem. Efforts should extend to international cooperation to address the global nature of cybercrimes and protect against the ever-evolving tactics employed by cybercriminals. Only through a comprehensive and collaborative approach can India effectively navigate the challenges posed by increasing cybercrimes and ensure a secure digital future for its citizens and organizations.

12.1 Recap of Key Takeaways

1. **Rapid Digitalization:** The surge in cybercrimes 1n India is closely linked to the rapid digitalization of the country. The increased use of technology, internet penetration, and digital platforms has created new opportunities for cybercriminals.

2. **Diverse Motives:** Cybercrimes in India are driven by diverse motives, including financial gain, hacktivism, espionage, revenge, thrill-seeking, and competitive advantage. Understanding these motives is crucial for developing targeted prevention and response strategies.

3. **Financial Fraud and Online Scams:** Financial motives remain a primary driver of cybercrimes in India. Online fraud, including phishing, identity theft, and various scams, has become prevalent, posing risks to individuals and businesses.

4. **Data Privacy Concerns:** Incidents of data breaches and leaks have raised significant concerns about data privacy in India. The need for robust data protection measures and legislation is evident in addressing these challenges.

5. **Legislative Framework and Cyber Laws:** India has enacted cyber laws, such as the Information Technology Act, to combat cybercrimes. However, the landscape continues to evolve, necessitating regular updates and enhancements to legal frameworks to keep pace with emerging threats.

6. **Global Threat Landscape:** India is not immune to global cyber threats. Incidents such as the WannaCry ransomware attack have demonstrated the interconnected nature of cyber threats, emphasizing the need for international collaboration in addressing cybersecurity challenges.

7. **Challenges in Law Enforcement:** Investigating and prosecuting cybercrimes pose challenges for law enforcement agencies in India. The transnational nature of many cybercrimes, coupled with the ability of cybercriminals to conceal their identities, requires sophisticated investigative approaches.

8. **Critical Infrastructure Vulnerabilities:** Instances of cyberattacks on critical infrastructure, such as the power outage in Mumbai, underscore the vulnerabilities in essential services. Securing critical infrastructure against cyber threats is a priority to ensure public safety and continuity of services.

9. **Awareness and Education:** Increasing awareness and education about cybersecurity are vital components of mitigating cybercrimes.

   Individuals and organizations need to be informed about best practices, potential threats, and measures to protect themselves from cyber threats.

10. **Government Initiatives:** The Indian government has initiated various cybersecurity programs, including the National Cyber Security Strategy. Collaborative efforts between government agencies, private sectors, and international partners are essential to strengthen the overall cybersecurity posture of the country.

11. **Technological Advancements and Emerging Threats:** As technology advances, so do cyber threats. Emerging technologies, such as artificial intelligence and the Internet of Things, present new challenges that require proactive measures to address potential vulnerabilities.

12. **Global Cybersecurity Standards:** Aligning with global cybersecurity standards and best practices is crucial. Adhering to international norms enhances India's cybersecurity resilience and facilitates cooperation with the global community.

In summary, the increasing cybercrimes in India necessitate a multifaceted approach involving legal, technological, educational, and collaborative efforts to mitigate risks, protect individuals and organizations, and create a secure digital environment for the nation.

12.2 The Importance of Cyber Vigilance in India's Digital Infrastructure.

Cyber vigilance holds paramount importance in safeguarding India's digital infrastructure, which has become the backbone of the nation's socio-economic fabric. As the country witnesses accelerated digitization and increased reliance on technology, the risks associated with cyber threats also escalate. Cyber vigilance involves a proactive and vigilant approach to monitoring, detecting, and Individuals and organizations need to be informed about best practices, potential threats, and measures to protect themselves from cyber threats.

1. **Government Initiatives:** The Indian government has initiated various cybersecurity programs, including the National Cyber Security Strategy. Collaborative efforts between government agencies, private sectors, and international partners are essential to strengthen the overall cybersecurity posture of the country.

2. **Technological Advancements and Emerging Threats:** As technology advances, so do cyber threats. Emerging technologies, such as artificial intelligence and the Internet of Things, present new challenges that require proactive measures to address potential vulnerabilities.

3. **Global Cybersecurity Standards:** Aligning with global cybersecurity standards and best practices is crucial. Adhering to international norms enhances India's cybersecurity resilience and facilitates cooperation with the global community.

In summary, the increasing cybercrimes in India necessitate a multifaceted approach involving legal, technological, educational, and collaborative efforts to mitigate risks, protect individuals and organizations, and create a secure digital environment for the nation.

12.2 The Importance of Cyber Vigilance in India's Digital Infrastructure.

Cyber vigilance holds paramount importance in safeguarding India's digital infrastructure, which has become the backbone of the nation's socio-economic fabric. As the country witnesses accelerated digitization and increased reliance on technology, the risks associated with cyber threats also escalate. Cyber vigilance involves a proactive and vigilant approach to monitoring,' detecting, and mitigating potential cyber threats and attacks. It is crucial in preserving the integrity, confidentiality, and availability of digital systems and data. With critical sectors such as finance, healthcare, energy, and governance becoming increasingly dependent on digital platforms, a breach in cybersecurity can have severe consequences, ranging from financial losses to threats to national security. By fostering a culture of cyber vigilance, India can fortify its digital infrastructure, protect sensitive information, and ensure the uninterrupted functioning of essential services. This necessitates continuous awareness campaigns, robust cybersecurity measures, regular updates to security protocols, and collaborative efforts between the government, private sector, and individuals to create a resilient and secure digital ecosystem.